The Christian as Minister

An Exploration Into the Meaning of God's Call to Ministry and the Ways The United Methodist Church Offers to Live Out That Call

Seventh Edition
2009

Sharon G. Rubey, editor
Contributors
Greg Hill
Meg Lassiat
Helen Neinast
Ciona Rouse
Anita Wood
Elliot Wright
Sandy Zeigler Jackson

Unless otherwise noted, scripture quotations are from the New Revised Standard Version Bible. Copyright © 1989 by the Division of Christian Education of the National Council of the Churches of Christ in the USA. Used by permission.

Disciplinary quotations are from *The Book of Discipline of the United Methodist Church* © 2008 by The United Methodist Publishing House. Used by permission.

Quotations taken from "Baptismal Covenants I, II, II-A," *The United Methodist Book of Worship* © 1976, 1980, 1985, 1989, 1992 by The United Methodist Publishing House are used by permission.

Produced by the Office of Interpretation and printed in the United States of America.

ISBN 978-0-938162-83-4

Cover design by Laura Deck, Office of Interpretation

Additonal copies of *The Christian as Minister* are available for $6.95 each from Cokesbury at 1-800-672-1789 or visit www.cokesbury.com.

The Christian as Minister

This resource is a compilation of information about the call to ministry and the avenues The United Methodist Church offers to live out that call. It is based in the concept of servant ministry and servant leadership presented by the Council of Bishops and affirmed by the General Conference (See ¶¶132-138, *2008 Book of Discipline.*)

Contents

Foreword

ALL CHRISTIANS ARE MINISTERS BY VIRTUE OF BEING INCORPORATED INTO THE CHURCH through baptism. This book is an introduction into the meaning of God's call to ministry, the vision for that ministry, and the opportunities The United Methodist Church offers to live out that call.

You will read about several opportunities for service and offices in the church as a lay person in chapter 2. You will also discover in that chapter a variety of ways that one may serve in ordained ministry. In this edition, two new sections have been written with emphases on God's call to young people, possible choices for exploring a response, and steps to follow in making a vocational choice.

Some of the positions for servant leadership on behalf of the church may be filled by either a lay or ordained person. Chapter 3 will outline steps and processes necessary to move into the roles described in this book.

As avenues for ministry, the positions are all related in that they offer the love of Christ to one another and the world in fulfilling the mission of the church. They are differentiated in their preparation for service, their structures of accountability, their length of commitment, and the specialized area of service.

Even though the General Board of Higher Education and Ministry has published this edition, *The Christian as Minister* would not have been complete without the cooperation and contribution of other general boards of The United Methodist Church which offer avenues and training for means of service in, and on behalf of, the church, both for lay and ordained ministries.

- Part of the General Board of Higher Education and Ministry's purpose is "preparing and assisting persons to fulfill their ministry in Christ in the several special ministries, ordained and diaconal; . . ." (¶1404, *2008 Book of Discipline*)
- The General Board of Discipleship purpose is to "help these persons to grow in their understanding of God that they may respond in faith and love . . . increasingly identifying themselves as children of God and members of the Christian community . . . to fulfill their common discipleship in the world. . . ." (¶1101, *2008 Book of Discipline*)
- The General Board of Global Ministries' responsibility in leadership is to "encourage and support the development of leadership in mission for both the Church and society." (¶1302.2, *2008 Book of Discipline*)

All Christians are connected through the Spirit of Christ. As members of Christ's body, the church, each of us is given various gifts "for the work of ministry, for building up the body of Christ." (Ephesians 4:4-16)

Categories of Servant Leadership Described in This Book

Lay Ministry Offices

- Lay Leader, who functions as the primary representative of the laity in the local church, district, or annual conference.
- Lay Missioner, trained to work in a team to develop faith communities.
- Lay Speaking Ministries, which give assistance and support to the program emphases of the church.
- Certified Lay Ministers, who enhance the quality of ministry and provide pastoral leadership, particularly to small membership churches.

Ordained Ministries

- Chaplains and Pastoral Counselors, who serve in specialized ministries of counseling.
- Deacons, who lead the church in the servanthood to which every Christian is called, relating the congregational life of the church to their ministries in the world.
- Elders, who lead the church in preaching, the sacraments, administration, and ordering the life of the church for mission.

Both Lay and Ordained Opportunities

- Commissioned Mission Service, in which people serve in several areas of missionary service, both nationally and internationally.
- Campus Ministers, who serve our United Methodist schools, colleges, and universities.

- Professional Certification Ministries, which are seven specialized areas of ministry in which people are professionally trained and certified.

Among the lay vocations in the church there are some who are serving in the consecrated lay ministry of diaconal ministers. The option for vocational service as a diaconal minister is no longer open to new candidates.

There are many settings where this resource may be useful besides an individual reading or a one-to-one conversation with a companion:

- High school, college, young adult, and adult groups could be guided through a vocational exploration process in Sunday, weekend, or retreat settings.
- College and university students may wish to explore the meaning of Christian vocation with a campus minister or a group of college students.
- Couples could read together and discuss what they learn from *The Christian as Minister*, since career and family decisions are often closely interrelated.
- The "Guidelines for Using the Text" and "Guidelines for the Pastor/Staff Parish Relations Committee" contained in chapters 4 and 5 of this book may be particularly helpful in understanding how to give proper support and guidance to candidates for ordained ministry.

In continuing the tradition of *The Christian as Minister*, it is the hope that this text will stimulate your mind and heart for an open and free exploration of God's call and your options for Christian service in The United Methodist Church.

Yours in ministry,
Sharon Rubey
Director of Candidacy and Conference Relations
Division of Ordained Ministry
General Board of Higher Education and Ministry
The United Methodist Church

Acknowledgments

SHARON RUBEY, DIRECTOR OF CANDIDACY AND CONFERENCE RELATIONS, GENERAL BOARD OF Higher Education and Ministry, has coordinated the revision of *The Christian as Minister*. We are grateful to the new Division on Ministries with Young People and the office of Laity in Ministry of the General Board of Discipleship, the Mission Personnel Program Area of the General Board of Global Ministries, and divisional representatives of the General Board of Higher Education and Ministry for their careful writing, review, and preparation of the text: Ciona Rouse, writing for the Division on Ministries with Young People; Sandy Jackson, Laity in Ministry; Elliot Wright, General Board of Global Ministries; Greg Hill, Anita Wood, and Sharon Rubey, Division of Ordained Ministry; Helen Neinast, Division of Higher Education, and Meg Lassiat, of both divisions of the General Board of Higher Education and Ministry. We are grateful for the many photographs provided by Mike DuBose of United Methodist Communications.

Our thanks are due also to the Office of Interpretation, specifically Terri Hiers, Henk Pieterse, and Vicki Brown for their editorial assistance, and Laura Deck for the layout and cover design; and to Richard A. Hunt, author of the first edition. Many of his thoughts and ideas were retained in this revision.

The Christian as Minister (ISBN 978-0-938162-83-4, $6.95 each) is available from Cokesbury at 1-800-672-1789 or visit www.cokesbury.com.

PAWNEE MISSION
INDIAN METHODIST
CHURCH

SUNDAY SCHOOL
10:00A.M.

WORSHIP SERVICE
11:00A.M.

EVERYONE WELCOME

Chapter One

The Christian Call to Servant Ministry

The Mission and Ministry of the Church

LIVING IN THE FIRST DECADE OF THE TWENTY-FIRST CENTURY HAS A COMPELLING QUALITY that evokes reflection on what has been and from where we have come. It also propels us forward to possibilities for the future and what can be.

To be sure, the time we live in intensifies our awareness of the changes, and the economic, social, and political forces that contribute to the complexity of our society. This complex diversity is a reality in our society and in our lives. The church is there for us to help us reflect about it and respond to it through the lens of our faith.

The church is where we learn about our faith, grow in it, and define our beliefs, which influence our actions, behaviors, and the way we live our lives. As a faith community, however, the church is not merely a human institution. It is the community where we also experience a relationship with God–a forgiving and transformative relationship founded on God's creative and unmerited love, the continuing redemptive grace of Jesus Christ, and the sustaining guidance of the Holy Spirit. Therefore, the church embodies both the ambiguities of life and the unquestionable continuing presence of Jesus the Christ.

The church is divine gift coupled with human response. The church cannot be seen apart from its community. That community, when it is faithful, transforms and liberates people and institutions from personal and social forms of

A member of Christ United Methodist Church in Columbus, Ohio, (left), and a Palestinian Muslim, light candles during the Interfaith Prayers for Peace worship service and rally.

sin. Freedom and transformation are the critical work of the church in our time–the mission and ministry of the church.

> *Rationale for Our Mission–The mission of the Church is to make disciples of Jesus Christ by proclaiming the good news of God's grace . . . thus seeking the fulfillment of God's reign and realm in the world. The fulfillment of God's reign and realm in the world is the vision Scripture holds before us. The United Methodist Church affirms that Jesus Christ is the Son of God, the Savior of the world, and the Lord of all. . . . We respect persons of all religious faiths and we defend religious freedom for all persons. Jesus' words in Matthew provide the Church with our mission: "Go therefore and make disciples of all nations, baptizing them in the name of the Father and of the Son and of the Holy Spirit, and teaching them to obey everything that I have commanded you. . . ." (28:19-20)*

> *This mission is our grace-filled response to the Reign of God in the world announced by Jesus. God's grace is active everywhere, at all times, carrying out this purpose as revealed in the Bible. It is expressed in God's covenant with Abraham and Sarah, in the Exodus of Israel from Egypt, and in the ministry of the prophets. It is fully embodied in the life, death, and resurrection of Jesus Christ. It is experienced in the ongoing creation of a new people by the Holy Spirit.*

> *John Wesley, Phillip Otterbein, Jacob Albright, and our other spiritual forbearers understood this mission in this way. Whenever United*

Methodism has had a clear sense of mission, God has used our Church to save persons, heal relationships, transform social structures, and spread spiritual holiness, thereby changing the world. In order to be truly alive, we embrace Jesus' mandate to . . . make disciples of all peoples. (¶121, 2008 Book of Discipline)

In the midst of our world community, beset by brokenness, the church offers a vision of peace, wholeness, and unity which God wills for all creation. It is this vision and this mission that gives the church focus and drive, and which invigorates and guides the church and its people.

Reflection

- In what ways have you experienced the church as a faith community in your life?
- In what ways have you experienced the church as a response to the societal and political forces which exclude, alienate, and marginalize?
- What is your understanding of the church's mission?

Baptism and Call

Baptism is God's gift of unmerited grace through the Holy Spirit. It is an incorporation into Christ which marks the entrance of each person into the church and its ministry. (Romans 6:3, 4, 18), (¶305, 2008 Book of Discipline)

The baptism liturgy tells us that "through baptism, (we) are incorporated by the Holy Spirit into God's new creation and made to share in Christ's royal priesthood."[1]

United Methodists believe young people, like adults, have a place among the people of God and are to be afforded the same holy privileges, regardless of age. When baptized as infants, children are to be nurtured in the faith and led to personal acceptance of Christ. Upon profession of faith in Christ, they confirm their baptism and acknowledge their place as growing disciples in the ministry of Christ.

This important aspect of the liturgy of the church serves to remind all that, through baptism and upon profession of faith–regardless of age, stage in life, or particular gifts and talents–our lives on this earth are to be visible extensions of the life and ministry of Jesus. We are the hands, the feet, the arms, the legs, the mind, the heart–the manifestation of Christ in this world.

The heart of Christian ministry is Christ's ministry of outreaching love.

Christian ministry is the expression of the mind and mission of Christ. . . . All Christians are called through their baptism to this ministry of servanthood in the world to the glory of God and for human fulfillment. The forms of this ministry are diverse in locale, in interest, and in denominational accent, yet always catholic in spirit and outreach. (¶125, 2008 Book of Discipline)

Through baptism we are acknowledged and incorporated into God's family and God's vision for a new creation and called to be a part of Christ's mission and ministry. The way each person responds to that call may lead to a time of reflection and deliberation about how God intends one to live out a Christian vocation. *Vocation* is defined by *The Random House College Dictionary* as a function or station in life to which one is called by God."[2]

The Gospel of Matthew chronicles the significance of Jesus' baptism and his relationship with God, and signals the beginning of his mission and ministry–his vocation.

And when Jesus had been baptized, just as he came up from the water, suddenly the heavens were opened to him and he saw the Spirit of God descending like a dove and alighting on him. And a voice from heaven said, "This is my Son, the Beloved, with whom I am well pleased." (Matthew 3:16-17)

The baptism of Jesus Christ was a significant act, because it publicly declared God's blessing and anointing. It was a commissioning–an empowering grace act through the work of the Holy Spirit. By virtue of our own baptism, we too are commissioned, anointed, and empowered to continue the ministry that Jesus started when he walked this earth. That makes all baptized persons ministers.

That God calls all to witness and service cannot be denied. However, the kind of witness and the kind of service to which God calls is a far more difficult question to answer.

Courtesy of U.S. Army Chaplain Corps

A U.S. Army chaplain preforms a baptism service for a military family. Military chaplains are called on to perform weddings and funerals, too.

This, again, is the question of vocation–the place where God's will for our lives and our obedience come together in the fulfillment of our purpose for being.

If you are exploring how God is calling you to live out Christ's ministry and vision, some of your anxiety may be addressed by looking carefully at the record of Jesus' struggle with his vocation and calling. There was a time in his life when Jesus did not know that he was to bear the history of God in a special way, a time when his vocation in life was not clearly understood. He struggled with who he was in relationship to God, and what it was that God intended for him to do. The agent of that discovery process was the Holy Spirit which, in his baptism, revealed Jesus to be the beloved Son of God and led him into the wilderness to struggle with what identity with God meant in the vocation to which he was being called.

Even after Jesus had clarified his calling, it was not always affirmed by the people of God. Listen to this account of his ministry in the synagogue at Nazareth.

When he came to Nazareth, where he had been brought up, he went to the synagogue on the Sabbath day, as was his custom. He stood up to read, and the scroll of the prophet Isaiah was given to him. He unrolled the scroll and found the place where it was written: "The Spirit of the Lord is upon me, because he has anointed me to bring good news to the poor. He has sent me to proclaim release to the captives and recovery of sight to the blind, to let the oppressed go free, to proclaim the year of the Lord's favor." And he rolled up the scroll, gave it back to the attendant, and sat down. The eyes of all in the synagogue were fixed on him. Then he began to say to them, "Today this scripture has been fulfilled in your hearing." All spoke well of him and were amazed at the gracious words that came from his mouth. They said, "Is not this Joseph's son?" He said to them, "Doubtless you will quote to me this proverb, 'Doctor, cure yourself!' And you will say, 'Do here also in your hometown the things that we have heard you did at Capernaum.'" And he said, "Truly I tell you, no prophet is accepted in the prophet's hometown . . . ." When they heard this, all in the synagogue were filled with rage. They got up, drove him out of the town, and led him to the brow of the hill on which their town was built, so that they might hurl him off the cliff. But he passed through the midst of them and went on his way. (Luke 4:16-24; 28-30)

The vocation of Jesus Christ was and is radically different than your vocation. Nevertheless, there is a relationship between his calling and yours. It is not accidental that you may be able to identify with elements in Jesus' baptism, wilderness journey, and ministry. His struggle with vocational choice was as real as yours.

In a way, your vocation in life grows out of his because, through the Holy Spirit, Christ is inviting you to share in God's story by witnessing to its reality in your life and living it out through your actions. Like Christ and the Apostles and the host of saints who have gone before you in the faith, you are called to discover the meaning of your vocation in the story-living and story-telling of the gospel. While the ways in which you tell it and the service you render in obedience to the will of God will differ from all others who surround you in the faith, you will find in that vocation, and only there, a true sense of who you are in relationship to God and who it is that you were meant to become. Gilbert Meilaender, professor of theology at Valparaiso University, writes in an article on vocation in the November 2000 edition of *The Christian Century*: "It is only by hearing, answering and participating in the divine calling that I can come to know who I am. We are not who we think we are; we are who God calls us to be."[3]

IsGodCallingYou.org

Discerning a call to ministry—ordained or otherwise—is an interactive process that involves talking with God, with other people, and with yourself. And it is a process, with many twists and turns along the way. Some people come to their calling more directly than others. They seem to know early on what God is calling them to be and do. God's creativity seems clear, straightforward. For others, the way is more circuitous, full of fits and starts, the kind of creativity that feels more like a roller coaster than a clear way forward. Whatever it's like for you right now, you'll find company. IsGodCallingYou.org is an interactive Web site that allows you to follow different paths for information on different forms of ministry. You'll find suggestions for prayer, people to talk to, things to read and resources geared specifically for you. Enter www.isgodcallingyou.org and see where your choices take you.

Reflection

- As part of the "family of Christ" signified by your baptism, what does being a "minister to the world in Christ's name" mean to you?
- What work would God have you do in the name of Christ, for the sake of the world?
- To what kind of ministry might God call you that could claim your total obedience?

Vocation and Servant Leadership [4]

Few people today enter the same occupation or line of work as their parents. Some drift into an occupation or follow the advice or pressure of parents or teachers or friends. The more deliberate may choose an occupation for themselves by considering what they do best or what they most enjoy doing. If they are systematic, they may consider the pros and cons of various trades or professions and study job listings to make a more systematic deliberate choice.

Responding to a call to a particular occupation or career or vocation is a fourth category of determining what one will do for one's lifework. Even though a call to a vocation might have elements of any of the preceding categories, it is also something above and beyond all of them.

This kind of call is not something a person responds to by default or under social pressure, or entirely by free choice. This call implies a caller. The Caller is God. *The Random House College Dictionary* lists as one definition of call: a "mystic experience of divine appointment to a vocation or service. . . ."[5] So determining one's vocation is more than fulfilling a personal dream; it is responding to God to become what God calls you to be. One gets to vocation through God's call.

The concept of a call by God can historically and biblically be applied to three distinct experiences.

- In the beginning, God called people into being. The word call is used here to refer to an important dimension of our relationship to God—a call that we share with all of humanity.
- Then God, through Jesus, calls persons to accept God's grace. People respond to this call by their commitment to Christ and his ministry. This is what binds us with all other Christians in the ministry of all believers.
- God also calls some persons to a particular form of servant leadership within the church. Empowered and guided by the Holy Spirit, these individuals respond to that call through a life-changing and often lifelong commitment to service and ministry.

The distinction between these calls, particularly the last two, is important. Every Christian is called to follow Christ in her or his walk of life wherever he or she is—the ministry of all believers. For persons who respond to a particular form of servant leadership, the word "call" expresses something that is uniquely different for each individual and something that hopefully leads to a vocation which theologian Frederick Buechner described as where one's greatest joy meets the world's greatest need.

Any type of call, sudden or gradual, needs a time of reflecting, questioning and testing. For further exploration of your call and its meaning for your vocation, talk with your pastor or another United Methodist minister or church leader.

The Meaning of Servant Leadership

Within The United Methodist Church, there are those called to servant leadership, lay and ordained. Such callings are evidenced by special gifts, evidence of God's grace, and promise of usefulness. God's call to servant leadership is inward as it comes to the individual and outward through the discernment and validation of the Church. The privilege of servant leadership is the call to share in the preparation of congregations and the whole Church for the mission of God in the world. The obligation of servant leadership is the forming of Christian disciples in the covenant community of the congregation. (¶137, 2008 Book of Discipline)

For these persons to lead the church effectively, they must embody the teachings of Jesus in servant ministries and servant leadership. (¶132, 2008 Book of Discipline)

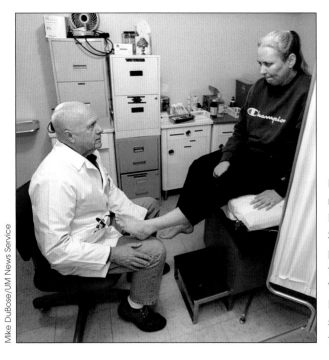

Mike DuBose/UM News Service

Dr. Earl J. Wipfler, a member of First United Methodist Church in St. Charles, Mo., sees a patient at the Volunteers in Medicine Clinic. Wipfler volunteers regularly at the clinic, which serves the uninsured in a two-county area.

Some might argue that servant leadership is a contradiction of terms. In order to explore the role of the servant leader more fully, look at the origin of the use of the term in our society and reflect on the most exemplary biblical servant leader of all time–Jesus Christ.

The term servant leadership was coined almost 30 years ago, in the business world, by Robert K. Greenleaf, director of Management Research at AT&T,

during the time of the Vietnam War, the political corruptness of Watergate, and Civil Rights unrest. His inspiration for this conception came from a novel by Hermann Hesse, a German poet and novelist, called *Journey to the East*.

"In this story we see a band of men on a mythical journey. . . . The central figure of the story is Leo who accompanies the party as the *servant* who does their menial chores, but who also sustains them with his spirit and his song. He is a person of extraordinary presence. All goes well until Leo disappears. Then the group falls into disarray and the journey is abandoned. They cannot make it without the servant Leo. The narrator, one of the party, after some years of wandering, finds Leo and is taken into the Order that had sponsored the [original] journey. There he discovers that Leo, whom he had known first as servant, was in fact the titular head of the Order, its guiding spirit, a great and noble leader."[6]

To Greenleaf, this story illustrated that "the great leader is seen as servant first." The difference between servant-first and leader-first "manifests itself in the care taken by the servant-first to make sure that other people's highest priority needs are being served. The best test is: do those served grow as persons; do they, *while being served*, become healthier, wiser freer, more autonomous."[7]

In most societies, including present day North American society, many people are socialized or programmed, as it were, to become either servants or leaders. Through cultural conditioning or through the operation of social structures some may be more predisposed to leadership roles, others to servant roles. Historically such a division has often been made on the basis of gender or ethnic group. In order to become a servant leader, a person must recognize her or his own predisposition. Those who see themselves as servants will need to learn to exercise leadership because in God's realm the effective servant often becomes a leader. Those who see themselves as leaders need to learn how to serve, because in God's realm the real leaders are those who serve most effectively.[8]

Servant Leadership in the Connectional Church

There is but one ministry in Christ, but there are diverse gifts and evidences of God's grace in the body of Christ (Ephesians 4:4-16). The ministry of all Christians is complementary. No ministry is subservient to another. All United Methodists are summoned and sent by Christ to live and work together in mutual interdependence and to be guided by the Spirit into the truth that frees and the love that reconciles. (¶130, 2008 Book of Discipline)

Through incorporation into the church, by baptism, people are connected to one another through Christ no matter what their role in ministry is. This con-

United Methodists gathered for General Conference 2008 in Fort Worth, Tex. Policy for the entire church is set during these meetings, which take place every four years.

Mike DuBose/UM News Service

nection shares a common tradition of faith, a common mission through Christ, and a common spirit that informs our beliefs and practices as United Methodists.

> *Connectionalism is an important part of our identity as United Methodists. . . . Our connectional system performs at least three essential tasks: embracing God's mission for the church . . . ; organizing our whole Church to enable local congregations, the primary arena for mission, faithfully and fruitfully to make disciples for Jesus Christ; and ensuring that all components in the connection carry out their appropriate responsibilities in ways that enable the whole United Methodist Church to be faithful in its mission. (¶701, 2008 Book of Discipline)*

> *The pattern for this connectional servant ministry is presented in the biblical beginning of the early church.*

The apostles led in prayer, teaching and preaching, ordered the spiritual and temporal life of the community, established leadership for the ministry of service, and provided for the proclamation of the gospel to new persons and in new places. The early church . . . set apart other persons to care for the physical needs of others, reflecting the concerns for the people of the world. In the New Testament (Acts 6), we see the apostles identifying and authorizing persons to a ministry of service. (¶302, 2008 Book of Discipline)

Our eighteenth century forebears in the faith reaffirmed the ancient Christian practices found in the early church even as they applied them anew in their own circumstances. Therefore, as many are called with diverse gifts, there are a variety of avenues of service and servant leadership in The United Methodist connectional structure.

Reflection

- What means are you using to discover the lifework or vocation that you believe God intends for you?
- Think of the ways you can lead people in your community or in your peer group to serve the needs that surround you.
- Do you feel that God may be calling you to be a servant leader? In what ways?
- What are questions that you have about different categories of ministry?

Notes

1. *The United Methodist Hymnal: Book of United Methodist Worship* (Nashville: The United Methodist Publishing House), p. 37.
2. *The Random House College Dictionary Revised Edition*, 1988, s.v. "vocation."
3. Gilbert Meilaender, "Divine Summons," in *The Christian Century*, November 2000 (Chicago: Christian Century Foundation), p. 1112.
4. Most of the following section is adapted from Simon Parker, *The Call to Servant Leadership* (Nashville: Division of Diaconal Ministry, General Board of Higher Education and Ministry, The United Methodist Church, 1998), pp. 7-8.
5. *The Random House College Dictionary Revised Edition*, 1988, s.v. "call."
6. Robert K. Greenleaf, *Servant As Leader* (Newton Center: Robert K. Greenleaf Center, 1973), p. 1.
7. Ibid., pp. 2, 7.
8. This paragraph is adapted from Simon Parker, *The Call to Servant Leadership*, pp. 19-20.

Chapter Two

Images of Servant Leadership

Young People in Ministry

EVERYBODY CAN BE GREAT, BECAUSE EVERYBODY CAN SERVE. YOU DON'T HAVE TO have a college degree to serve. You don't have make your subject and your verb agree to serve. You don't have to know about Plato and Aristotle to serve. You don't have to know Einstein's "Theory of Relativity" to serve. You don't have to know the Second Theory of Thermal Dynamics in Physics to serve. You only need a heart full of grace, a soul generated by love, and you can be that servant.
                                       –The Rev. Dr. Martin Luther King Jr. *

All members of Christ's universal church are called to share in the ministry which is committed to the whole church of Jesus Christ. . . .This servanthood is performed in family life, daily work, recreation and social activities, responsible citizenship, the stewardship of property and accumulated resources, the issues of corporate life, and all attitudes toward other persons. (¶220, 2008 Book of Discipline*)*

God's call takes many forms and people hear God's call differently; therefore, people find many different ways to respond to God's call. Because we are

---

* The Rev. Dr. Martin Luther King Jr., "The Drum Major Instinct" (sermon delivered at Ebenezer Baptist Church, Atlanta, Ga., February 1968).

United Methodist youths share Holy Communion during a Warmth in Winter youth event in Nashville, Tenn. Young people, like all Christians, are called to God's ministry in the church and the world.

called, God shows us places and ways to serve. The only requirement is being available to God and answering God's call.

"Ben" was traveling with his sixth grade confirmation class the week-end after the September 11, 2001, terrorist attacks on the World Trade Center. Overwhelmed by his desire to help children whose parents had been injured or killed, he suggested sending stuffed animals to these children as one way to provide comfort. Ben shared his idea with the other confirmation students and they decided to help. Members of the class talked with students at several local schools and announced the need for stuffed animals at church, through church mailings, and on the church Web site. For the next two weeks, stuffed animals were collected, both at the schools and at the church. When the class met to sort the toys and ship them to New York, they discovered more than 1,000 stuffed animals had been collected! They were given to law enforcement officers and social workers to share with children most directly affected by the attacks.

At age 16, "Tiffany" was the president of her youth group. She was a leader among her peers and also attended a number of church council meetings. Both youth and adult members of the congregation admired and followed Tiffany's leadership. One day the pastor at her church asked to meet so that they could discuss Tiffany's ministry. At their meeting, the pastor said, "I'm so glad that you've decided to be a minister!" A look of concern crossed Tiffany's face. I never told Rev. Williams I'd be a minister, Tiffany thought. Doesn't she know I want to be a doctor? Besides, I'm only 16. I don't feel called to be a minister. Noticing Tiffany's confusion, Rev. Williams further explained, "When we take our baptism seriously and follow God's call to be a disciple of Jesus Christ, we are ministers–regardless of age, gender or our career plans. You may be called to be a pastor like I am, or your ministry may be in the hospital like you dream. Either way, I'm excited that you've been called to serve!"

As "Carol" boarded the plane to leave on her second trip to Zimbabwe, she couldn't help but reflect on what the last year had meant for her. During the summer between her junior and senior years in high school, she traveled to Zimbabwe with her church's youth group to work with children at the Fairfield Orphanage in Old Mutare, Zimbabwe. While at the orphanage Carol played with the children, shared laughter and smiles with them, and developed relationships with the adult workers– relationships that continued to make an impression on her once she returned to the United States. She knew she would return to Mutare. Carol shared the story of her time in Zimbabwe with friends at her high school and soon decided to lead a trip back there so her friends could see and experience some of the same things she had. Eighteen other classmates and friends joined the group and they began preparations for their upcoming trip. Carol organized the trip, made travel arrangements, and worked tirelessly helping the group to raise funds. She stayed in contact with the people at Fairfield and planned what the group would do during their visit. Additionally, she worked with her school administrators to establish an ongoing sponsorship program. She learned a lot in the process and knew she was making a difference–not only with the children at the Fairfield Orphanage, but with her friends who would soon get to meet the people at Fairfield and experience Zimbabwe firsthand. She was excited to return and knew this would not be the last time she would visit.

It is certainly clear that Mary, the mother of Jesus, had no intention to be used by God in such an amazing way. It probably never crossed her young mind that she would have a son who could be one of the teachers in the temple, or a traveling pastor. Not to mention that she would be an instrument to help change the world. Yet, when God called on her to carry and give birth to Jesus, her response was: "Here am I, the servant of the Lord; let it be with me according to your word." (Luke 1:38) Without ordination or formal education, Mary, at a young age, became God's servant and answered God's call.

This ministry of all Christians in Christ's name and spirit is both a gift and a task. The gift is God's unmerited grace; the task is unstinting service. Entrance into the church is acknowledged in baptism and may include persons of all ages. (¶128, 2008 Book of Discipline*)*

When you join the church, you answer a call from God. You say "yes" to God's grace, to becoming part of a community of Christians, and to serving others on behalf of Jesus Christ.

Reflection

- What image comes to your mind when you ask: How is God calling me to respond as a baptized Christian?
- What does servant leadership mean to you as a young person in school?
- What experiences have you had that may influence the way you answer a call from God which may lead to a vocation in the church?

Volunteer Susan Polk works in the garden at Camp Dogwood near Ashland City, Tenn. Produce raised there will be brought to town and sold at two local churches.

The Ministry of the Laity
The Call

The heart of Christian ministry is to share Christ's love in the world. The ministry of the laity is a frontline ministry because lay people have direct access to the community and the world through their secular jobs and activities.

All of the people of God are called to be faithful in their ministry. Church members are the church made visible in the world and "must convince the world of the reality of the gospel or leave it unconvinced." (¶129, *2008 Book of Discipline*) This responsibility cannot be delegated nor can it be evaded. If Christians are not faithful in ministry, the church will lose its impact on the world.

As members of the body of Christ, we are all are gifted for service. "Now there are a variety of gifts, but the same Spirit . . ." (1 Corinthians 12:4-7) and "The ministry of all Christians is complementary. No ministry is subservient to another." (¶130, *2008 Book of Discipline*)

It is liberating to realize that each one of us is called to ministry and that each one's ministry is just as important as the other's. It is essential to realize this important fact and live out ministry as we have been gifted and called–whether it is in the factory, or the hospital; at work or at home; in the church, or in the community. Christ has called and we answer by serving to the best of our ability.

Privilege and Responsibility

The call to ministry is both a privilege and a responsibility. We are privileged to be in relationship with God. It is a privilege to be part of a "holy nation, a royal priesthood, one of God's own people" because we have been "called out of darkness into God's marvelous light." (1 Peter 2:9) And it is a privilege to "proclaim the mighty acts of God."

It is also a responsibility. Christians respond to God's call by holy living and obedience to Christ. Holy living inspires intentional growth and nurturing. Each must continue to grow spiritually, to mature in the Christian life in order to fully engage in the ministry of all Christians. (See ¶¶134, 135, and 136, *2008 Book of Discipline.*)

John Wesley established The General Rules for the Societies who met together to pray, worship, and watch over one another in love. These rules included ways to accomplish the task of loving and serving others. First, by doing no harm, by avoiding evil of every kind. Second, by doing good of every possible sort, and as far as possible to all persons. Third, by attending upon all the ordinances of God which are the practices by which we stay connected to God, grow in faith and in the ability to love–the means of grace. (See General Rules pp. 72-74, *2008 Book of Discipline.*)

What does servant leadership look like in an everyday life?

Here are a few examples:

"Naomi" is a nurse who has felt God's call on her life. She lives out that call in her work every day trying to treat her co-workers, supervisor and patients the way Jesus would treat them. She goes out of her way to perform acts of kindness and she offers to pray for people she meets who are hurting. Outside the workplace she seeks ways to grow spiritually through prayer, Bible study and worship, and to develop the sense of call in her life. Because of her deepened spirituality she has the courage to pray with patients and co-workers as well as **for** them. She volunteers to visit members of the church who are homebound or in the hospital. She has started a prayer ministry in her church to help others realize the power and importance of prayer.

"Brian" works as an electrician. He finds ways to befriend others, share his faith story, and invite them to church. Brian is obedient to Christ in his daily life by showing concern for his fellow workers. He refuses to cut corners or be dishonest with his employer. Brian walks the talk. Outside of work he is active in prison ministry and serves as a volunteer at the local prison in order to make a difference in the lives of the inmates and prison personnel. At his church he leads a team to provide a free meal for the community on Christmas day with turkey and all the trimmings. He also leads mission trips to poverty stricken areas of the country and to other nations and uses his skills to improve their quality of life.

"Beth" has a full-time job as wife and mother. Her ministry in daily life is providing nourishing meals, clean laundry, and living conditions for her family. She sees this as her service to God. She has taken a leadership role in her district and annual conference where she teaches classes to help other laity improve their leadership and ministry skills. Her leadership encourages people to be involved by using their skills to help the less fortunate. This has led many people to serve in community ministries such as serving lunch at the homeless shelter or delivering Meals on Wheels. It is important to Beth to make people feel welcome in her church so she often serves as a greeter at worship services.

"Lee" is a business executive who ministers in his work by using ethical practices in his company and dealing honestly with his employees and customers. Lee devotes time in the community to coaching a Little League baseball team. His coaching is an example to other coaches of Christ's love for children. As a member of the finance committee at his church, Lee tries to ensure that the meetings are more than church business, that the meetings are times for holy conferencing and Christian fellowship. He is part of a covenant group that meets weekly. This group prays for each other and holds each other accountable for their discipleship.

All of these people are in vital ministry. They are examples of servant ministry and leadership in their daily work lives, their families, communities, churches, and in the world.

When the Son of Man comes in his glory, and all the angels with him, then he will sit on the throne of his glory. All the nations will be gathered before him, and he will separate the people one from another as a shepherd separates the sheep from the goats, and he will put the sheep at his right hand and the goats at the left. Then the king will say to those at his right hand, "Come, you that are blessed by my Father, inherit the kingdom prepared for you from the foundation of the world; for I was hungry and you gave me food, I was thirsty and you gave me something to drink, I was a stranger and you welcomed me, I was naked and you gave me clothing, I was sick and you took care of me, I was in prison and you visited me." Then the righteous will answer him, "Lord, when was it that we saw you hungry and gave you food, or thirsty and gave you something to drink? And when was it that we saw you a stranger and welcomed you, or naked and gave you clothing? And when was it that we saw you sick or in prison and visited you?" And the king will answer them, "Truly I tell you, just as you did it to one of the least of these who are members of my family, you did it to me." (Matthew 25:31-40)

Reflection

- How have you been obedient to the call to servant ministry?
- In what ways can you invest your time and talents for ministry in the name of Christ?
- What opportunities do you have in your everyday life to be in ministry?

The Ministry of the Deacon

Within the people of God, some persons are called to the ministry of deacon. The words deacon, deaconess, and diaconate all spring from a common Greek root–diakonos, or "servant", and diakonia, or "service." Very early in its history the church . . . instituted an order of ordained ministers to personify or focus the servanthood to which all Christians are called. These people were named deacons. This ministry exemplifies and leads the Church in the servanthood every Christian is called to live both in the church and the world. The deacon embodies the interrelationship between worship in the gathered community and service to God in the world. (¶305, 2008 Book of Discipline)

From among the baptized, deacons are called by God to a lifetime of servant leadership authorized by the Church, and ordained by a bishop.

Deacons fulfill servant ministry in the world and lead the Church in relating the gathered life of Christians to their ministries in the world. . . . [They] give leadership in the Church's life: in the teaching and proclamation of the Word; in worship, and in assisting the elders in the administration of the sacraments of baptism and the Lord's Supper; in forming and nurturing disciples; in conducting marriages and burying the dead; in the congregation's mission to the world; and in leading the congregation in interpreting the needs, concerns, and hopes of the world. (¶328, 2008 Book of Discipline)

The role of the ordained deacon in full connection is as diverse as the world's needs. Following in the long history of diaconal workers, a deacon's call to word and service is lived out in a variety of ways. But it is always focused on providing servant leadership in one or more of the following:

- Leading the church in its servant ministry by the formation of disciples and connectional outreach.
- Giving leadership to a direct service ministry beyond the local church.
- Giving leadership in worship and assisting in the ministry of the sacraments.
- Teaching and proclaiming the word directly or living out the word of Jesus' love and justice through action and deed.

Deacons serve in multiple settings:
- a local church
- a social service agency affiliated with the UMC
- a general agency of the church
- an organization or ministry beyond the local church that responds to the needs of the community.

What is common in deacon service is that the person is accountable to the annual conference and the bishop, and also to their primary setting in ministry. They must also commit to equip themselves through theological education and train to serve in a specialized area of ministry. And no matter where they serve, ordained deacons will always be affiliated with a local congregation helping to lead them in their servant ministry.

Deacons Serving in A Variety of Ministry Settings

"Judith's" passion for mission work dominates her work as deacon associate at a local United Methodist Church. She helps oversee the 4,000-member church's adult ministries, including helping to lead a contemporary worship service, planning events and stewardship campaigns, organizing Bible studies and small-group ministries, and leading 260 singles ranging in age from 24 to 82 representing at least eight denominations. Divided into older and younger groups, the singles ministry offers Sunday morning classes, social activities, weekly Bible studies, retreats, and mission opportunities. With her support and guidance, the singles ministry and church-at-large has supported missionaries, traveled to Costa Rica and Mexico on mission trips, provided necessities for a nearby family shelter, collected items for the Society of Saint Stephens, and built homes for private sector initiatives.

"Mary" is a deacon in full connection who has combined her training as a counselor with theological education to respond to her call to ministry. She serves as director of a crisis intervention center and believes that her work is an extension of the ministry of Jesus Christ and therefore of the church. In her office, she deals with crisis phone calls from people who are suffering with depression or who face problems in their lives and need to talk with someone who shows care and concern. She is committed to connecting the needs of the community and the gifts and talents of the congregation where she is serving.

The area of health care is the setting for "Naomi's" ministry. She serves and fulfills her call as deacon as a parish nurse. At this time in history there are many older adults who need the services of a nurse. Naomi combines her licensed nursing skills with pastoral care and theological education to become a presence of the Body of Christ, the church, with the people.

"Jim" has responded to the call to be a deacon as a social worker with seminary training who serves as the director of a children's home which is a United Methodist agency. This agency has become a major provider of foster care for children who have been abandoned or have been physically or sexually abused. Jim notes that it is in the midst of suffering and oppression that the embodiment of the ministry of Jesus Christ needs to be present. He is connected with not one, but all the churches in the area, to interpret the tremendous need that exists in our society to give hope to our children. He incarnates the passage of Matthew 25:40–"Truly I tell you, just as you did it to one of the least of these . . . you did it to me."

"Dean" has been appointed as deacon to coordinate and mobilize a local church outreach ministry. His ministry is to survey the community needs and determine how the congregation can respond to those needs. He has surveyed the congregation to determine the gifts, talents, and abilities to make a significant presence and difference in the community by involving those at church in the homeless program, hospice program, Meals on Wheels, respite care, Habitat for Humanity, prison ministries, halfway houses, shelter for battered women, and the care program for patients with AIDS. He sees the importance of the interrelatedness of the community and the congregation. His call to the diaconate is to bring into reality John Wesley's statement, "The world is my parish."

"Joan" says she is called by God to minister with individuals who believe God does not love them. She started a ministry with pregnant women to serve as a conduit of grace to comfort the spirit, nurture hope and represent the presence of a loving God within a multi-cultural, ecumenical environment. Joan ministers to pregnant women who are incarcerated by helping them work through their grief and anger at not

Vicki Brown/GBHEM

Communion is celebrated during EXPLORATION 2006 in Jacksonville, Fla.

being able to raise their newborns. She acts as their labor buddy, chaplain and "mother" as they go through labor and delivery. To connect the world of the prison and the church, the congregation where Joan serves as minister of reconciliation sends pink or blue baby Bibles and letters of encouragement to the inmates and to the babies' caregivers. She also serves as chaplain and spiritual director to adolescent girls in residential treatment facilities. Congregational members transport the girls to worship service weekly. Joan and her congregation provide a ministry of care with families who have experienced the loss of a baby within the first 20 weeks of pregnancy. An annual memorial service is held at the church. Joan is fulfilling the ministry of the deacon by connecting the hurting needs in the world with the response of the church.

Reflection

- It has been said that the scope of ministry for deacons is determined by the needs in society. To know the needs one must prayerfully read the signs of the times. As you read the newspapers and watch and listen to the news, what are some of the signs in your community and in the world that reflect areas of ministry in which deacons might serve?
- How does the ministry of the deacon reflect servant ministry and servant leadership?
- Do you have gifts, talents and/or interests that reflect the specialized ministry of a deacon? What are some of them?
- How might these special gifts, talents or interests be used as a deacon on behalf of the church in the service of Christ's mission and ministry?

The Pastoral Ministry of Elders and Local Pastors

Those whose leadership in service includes preaching and teaching the Word of God, administration of the sacraments, ordering the church for its mission and service, and administration of the Discipline *of the church are ordained as elders. (¶303.2, 2008* Book of Discipline*)*

All persons not ordained as elders who are appointed to preach and conduct divine worship and perform the duties of a pastor shall have a license for pastoral ministry." (¶315, 2008 Book of Discipline*)*

In The United Methodist Church, a pastoral charge consists of one or more local churches or congregations to which an ordained or licensed pastor is appointed as lead pastor. In larger churches there may be additional ordained elders or licensed personnel appointed as associates. In some communities of faith, the pastor in charge may participate in a team ministry that includes local pastors, associate members, deacons, and laity. In other instances, two pastors may be appointed as co-pastors of a church or charge. Sometimes several local churches form a cooperative parish, group ministry, or extended parish that has a staff including more than one ordained minister and other paid staff persons. The paid church staff of larger churches or cooperative parishes may include administrators, educators, music and age-group specialists, and others who provide services to congregation and community. Some of these persons may be diaconal ministers; others may be mission personnel of the General Board of Global Ministries.

Whether the parish is large or small, the tasks of the licensed or ordained minister who is a pastor are similar. Consider, for a moment, the responsibilities of a pastor as outlined below.

> *The responsibilities of elders and licensed pastors are derived from the authority given in ordination and licensing. Elders have a fourfold ministry of Word, Sacrament, Order, and Service within the connection and thus serve in the church and the world. Local pastors share with the elders the responsibilities and duties of a pastor for this fourfold ministry. (¶340, 2008 Book of Discipline)*

In the context of this fourfold ministry, a pastor gives attention to the following duties:

1. Word and ecclesial acts
   - preaching the Word of God and teaching the Scriptures
   - personal, ethical, and spiritual counseling
   - ecclesial acts of marriage and burial
   - visiting the community of faith, the sick, aged, imprisoned, and others in need
2. Sacrament
   - administering the sacraments of baptism and the Lord's Supper
   - encouraging the private and congregational use of other means of grace
3. Order
   - being the administrative officer
   - administering the temporal affairs of the church
   - participating in denominational and conference programs
   - leading the congregation in racial and ethnic inclusiveness

The Rev. HiRho Park blesses the Communion elements at Salem United Methodist Church in Hebbville, Maryland.

4. Service

- embodying the ministry of Jesus in servant ministries and servant leadership
- giving leadership in ordering the congregation for ministry in the world
- building the body of Christ as a caring and giving community
- participating in community, ecumenical, and interreligious concerns

Pastors vary widely in their interests, skills, and attitudes. These characteristics, combined with the needs of the parish, lead pastors to devote quite different proportions of time to the major tasks of the pastor described above. Though the pastors of large churches may specialize in one or two of these basic areas of responsibility, most pastors must attend to all of the duties while, at the same time, caring for their own personal needs and the needs of their families. The following stories will give you insight into the ways these duties are lived out in a variety of settings.

A Journal of Pastoral Ministries

Sunday: "John" is a recent seminary graduate appointed as an associate pastor of a large suburban church. He was up earlier than usual this morning because it was one of the few Sundays of the year that he would preach at the 8:30 a.m. and 11:00 a.m. worship services. Normally, his participation in worship is limited to the reading of scripture or a prayer. Though preaching, he still led a young adult class during the Sunday school hour and met with the youth in the evening. At the end of this busy day, Tim, a leader in the youth group, wanted to discuss how to help a friend with a problem. John spent the afternoon with his family.

Monday: A clergy couple, "Doug" and "Sandy", is assigned to a rural circuit. After breakfast, they worked on the worship plans for the coming Sunday and reviewed their busy schedule for the week. While Sandy read some background material for her sermon, Doug prepared a column for the church newsletter. Their work together was cut short when Sue came by to ask Doug's help in finding a convalescent home for her 86-year-old mother. After lunch, Sandy visited several members in the hospital, while Doug contacted the director of a United Methodist home to find out what options were open to Sue and her mother. After dinner, Doug had a meeting at church, while Sandy relaxed after a busy day.

Tuesday: "Rod" is the pastor of a growing urban African-American congregation. Early in the morning, he was out of the parsonage sitting on the bench at the bus stop talking with people as they left for work. By discovering who they were and what they did, he had an opportunity to do some street counseling and introduce them to the ministry of the church. By 8:00 a.m., he was at the hospital with the Jacksons during Mr. Jackson's surgery. The family had a lot of questions about hospital procedures, death, and faith. This was his first opportunity to become better acquainted with this family. He returned to the church office about 10:30 a.m. and completed plans for the Sunday service. Rod had lunch with a committee working on ways to get tutoring services for children who are not sufficiently served by the existing public school programs. Later in the day, he saw a man who needed help getting a job, a couple who are going through divorce, and a teenager who thinks she is pregnant.

Wednesday: "Juanita" is a local pastor of a small Hispanic congregation trying to establish itself in a satellite city of a major metropolitan area. The Spanish language population of the city has grown rapidly as migrant workers, immigrants, and transient families settled into this relatively small urban area. In the middle of the morning, Juanita met with the personnel manager of a local factory to see if there were any jobs open for the unemployed of her community. There were a few jobs, menial in nature and paying minimum wages. In the afternoon, she walked through the neighborhood talking with the people she saw. She uncovered more needs than she could ever hope to address. She was joined by her lay leader that evening, and together they sat down with the board of trustees of the church which allows them to share facilities. There is frustration over the additional maintenance costs of housing two congregations in the same building. Juanita yearns for the day when her congregation can have a church building of its own.

Thursday: "Linda" is the pastor of a small-town church. After getting her youngest child off to school, she headed for a meeting with the other pastors of the district. They discussed special offerings and plans for a lay leadership training program and then were addressed by an interdenominational panel of clergy on the ecumenical concerns of the area. During lunch, Linda received word that Mr. Young had died and the funeral would be on Saturday afternoon. She left the luncheon early and went directly to the Young residence. Sandra Young and the children were upset and needed Linda's support and prayers, so she stayed with them the rest of the afternoon. After dinner with her family, she met with the team of visitors who would go to the homes of new residents, visitors to the church, the sick, and the bereaved. Their awareness of Mr. Young's death made them more sensitive to the importance of their tasks.

Friday: "George" is an ordained elder on a parish ministry team. He began this morning as he has most Friday mornings, completing his preparations for the Sunday service. His review of the service was cut short, however, by the arrival of other members of the leadership team. They spent the next several hours evaluating their work in the parish, sharing mutual concerns, and discussing how to do a better job with people facing crises. Their meeting concluded with lunch. George enjoys the support he gets from other members of the team. He can't imagine effective parish ministry without it. George did some running in the late afternoon and spent the entire evening with his family. Though he received several phone calls around dinner, he scheduled appointments for the coming week with those who wished to see him.

Saturday: "Paul" is a Korean pastor who is working hard to develop a small congregation in a metropolitan area. He was up early, as usual, and began the day in prayer with his family. They prayed for one another, the church, the needs of its members, and the world. After breakfast Paul read a little, reworked a section of his sermon and made copies of the Sunday bulletin. He then spent a few hours calling on church members before returning to the church for an afternoon youth meeting. Soon after the youth left the church, a young couple arrived with their friends and family to rehearse a wedding which would take place on Sunday afternoon. After a rehearsal dinner, Paul had time to spend with his preschooler before he put her to bed. Paul and his wife have adapted to their work schedules by looking to the middle of the week for the family time they often miss on weekends.

Reflection

- How does the ministry of a pastor with its multiple responsibilities and opportunities relate to the gifts you might bring to this ministry? Or do you see no relationship?
- How is pastoral ministry complimentary to lay ministry within the local church?

Chaplaincy and Pastoral Counseling

If you did not already know, you have discovered by reading this book that United Methodist clergy can serve God's people in places other than United Methodist congregations. Did you know that deacons, elders, and licensed local pastors can also serve as pastoral counselors or chaplains?

Deacons, elders, and local pastors can serve in ministries of pastoral care in specialized settings. Deacons, elders, associate members, and provisional members may be endorsed after completing the requirements. Licensed local pastors may be granted associate status by the United Methodist Endorsing Agency. *(See ¶1421.5, 2008 Book of Discipline.)*

A primary difference between these appointments and the local church is the nature of the institution in which ministry takes place and the role of the clergy in that institution. Some of the institutions where chaplains serve include hospitals, hospice, prisons, industry, the workplace, and the military services. Pastoral counselors are found in private practice as well as on the staff of pastoral counseling centers.

Many times, chaplains and pastoral counselors serve institutions that are culturally diverse and multidisciplinary. While chaplains perform traditional functions such as rites, sacraments, ordinances, pastoral care and religious education, they also perform nontraditional roles. Two of those include: advising the institutional leadership on ethics and the impact of decisions on people and performing administration to enable ministries of excellence using other than church funds and processes.

Descriptions of Chaplains and Pastoral Counselors

Hospital Chaplains

Every day, hospital chaplains help patients and their relatives cope with sickness, disability, and even death. In mental hospitals, the problems are perhaps even more excruciating. Chaplains in these settings are part of a team. They work shoulder to shoulder with doctors, nurses, psychiatrists, and social workers.

The role of the chaplain is to provide pastoral care for patients' families and for staff. They reach out to those on the wards and in the surgery and critical care waiting rooms. Generally, they will be on ethics committees as they deal with complex issues of modern medicine. They frequently lead Bible studies and conduct worship services in hospital chapels.

Prison Chaplains

"I was in prison and you visited me. . . ." (Matthew 25:36) In the correctional setting (prisons, jails, detention facilities), chaplains have the opportunity to pastor unique and diverse communities, in both traditional and nontraditional ways. They preach, teach, baptize, serve Holy Communion, counsel, visit, and serve the prisoner congregation. They are pastors not only to inmates, but also to the staff and the families of both communities. They serve and are available to all the people incarcerated in their institution, providing for spiritual needs regardless of religious affiliation. This involves recruiting, training, and supervising a broad variety of religious volunteers from surrounding communities. They serve as a link between the religious communities on the outside and those on the inside, helping to build bridges of care and service both ways.

Industry/Workplace Chaplains

The success of industry is measured by the rate of production and flow of profit. The industrial chaplain stands in the middle of the needs of management and those of the men and women who power the industrial machine. When these people arrive on the job, they bring with them everything that is going on in their lives–from the joy of a firstborn baby to a nagging problem with alcohol–and inevitably it affects their job performance.

Chaplains provide a ministry to people in business and industry, responding to individual and family needs as well as work-life concerns such as job stress and career. They provide a preventative, as well as a problem-solving ministry, that reaches out with a concern for all people.

Chaplains work with industrial management at a number of levels. They frequently train supervisors on the line to relate more effectively to their workers who appear to be suffering from a personal problem. The chaplain is also influential at the policy level, conferring with management when new policies are proposed. Individual counseling often leads to referrals to in-house programs or community social services.

Military Chaplains

The role of the military chaplain is not to justify war, but to minister to the spiritual needs of service men and women and their families in a unique setting. Military chaplains are never asked to violate the tenets of their own faith as they work in a pluralistic arena in both war and peace. The chaplain trains with

Workplace and military chaplains provide counseling and pastoral care outside the walls of the traditional church.

the service members and prepares to be spiritually, mentally, and physically ready to go wherever and whenever service members are deployed world-wide.

The chaplain serves on the staff of the commander and has ready access to service members on flight lines, in motor pools, on ships, and in the field environment. On military posts and bases, worship services are conducted in beautifully appointed chapels with ongoing weekday ministries in the chapels or family-life centers. The United Methodist Church endorses chaplains for full-time, active duty, as well as for reserve component duty, concurrent with local church or other specialized ministry.

Pastoral Counselors

While it is true that all pastors counsel people, pastoral counselors endorsed by the United Methodist Endorsing Agency have undergone additional specialized training so they can integrate resources of scripture and faith with insights from the behavioral sciences. Pastoral counselors serve on staffs of local churches, in pastoral counseling centers, in health care institutions, or in private practice.

The Uniqueness of Ministry Endorsed by the United Methodist Endorsing Agency

Clergy endorsed by the United Methodist Endorsing Agency operate in culturally and religiously diverse settings. They serve people who may or may not be United Methodists. Yet strangely, there is identification with the chaplain or pastoral counselor if he or she is credible and relevant to the needs of the individual within that institution.

Many times, the ministry takes place with clergy from other faith groups such as Roman Catholic, Jewish, Muslim, Orthodox, or other Protestants. Each chaplain is required to provide religious support which consists of rites, sacraments, ordinances, pastoral care, and religious education within their faith group, or to coordinate for someone else to accommodate a belief system that conflicts with their own.

Chaplains are expected to be both pastoral and prophetic to the institution. Sometimes, chaplains are required to advise the institutional leadership on ethics and the impact of decisions on people.

Unlike the local church, coordinating resources for ministry is done within the administrative processes of another institution. The coordination may require securing a place for religious activities, funds, and other resources such as transportation, supplies, equipment, and even permission for people to be free to attend certain events.

- Do you sense a call to a particular extension ministry of the church?
- What specific gifts, training, education, and work experience do you bring to the unique requirement of this specialized ministry?
- Can you work collegially with clergypersons of other religious bodies to provide for pastoral care of all persons?

Higher Education Campus Ministry

Settings and Personnel

The United Methodist Church is in ministry on more than 700 college and university campuses in the U.S. These represent many kinds of ministry settings.

- Some are Wesley Foundations (United Methodist Campus Ministry sites funded in large part by annual conference budgets.)
- Others are ecumenical ministries (cooperating in the name of United Methodism with one or more denominations which share funding responsibilities.)
- Some campus ministries are staffed by chaplains at United Methodist-related or other private universities and colleges. (These are funded by the school itself.)

At independent or church-related colleges and universities, the chaplain may be part of the student-affairs office or the religion department. Or, the chaplain may report directly to the president's office. Church-related institutions usually provide on-campus space for the chaplain's office and activities.

At public colleges and universities, the campus ministry may be located adjacent to the campus in a church-owned building although schools sometime provide space on the campus itself. Campus ministers at commuter and community colleges may not be campus based at all, but may work out of local churches or offices in their homes. They do much of their ministry within the context of the community college's own cycle of activities.

Some campus ministers and chaplains are ordained elders and deacons; others are not.

Did you know John Wesley was a campus minister? In the early eighteenth century, he and his brother, Charles, started the Holy Club at Oxford University in England. And ever since, United Methodists have been in ministry on campuses.

Some work full time on campus; others are part time. Campus ministers who are ordained are both employed by a college, university, or ecumenical agency, and are appointed by and accountable to the bishop of their annual conference.

Of the more than 700 colleges and universities served by The United Methodist Church, the campuses and student bodies also vary dramatically.

- One campus minister develops programs on a small residential campus where students are quite accessible, since they live and work on campus.
- Another works on a large, urban, commuter campus where students spend little time on the campus, either before or after classes.
- Still another may serve a sprawling university campus where students of all ages have a variety of lifestyles and live in a variety of situations, both on campus and off.

> The United Methodist Campus Ministers Association was created in the summer of 2005 to empower campus ministers to lead thriving ministries, to interpret the mission and ministry of campus ministry to the wider church, to provide for excellence in leadership in campus ministry, and to provide resources for personal and professional growth for those in higher education ministry.

The Ministry on the Campus

For all these settings, ministry with students is a central emphasis. But campus ministers and chaplains are also concerned with faculty, staff, and administrators. As the name implies, campus ministry is a ministry to the whole campus.

Campus ministry could be 200 people gathered for a weekend conference examining sexuality from sociological, psychological, and theological perspectives. It could mean a lively discussion about religion and the arts, or about religion and the anatomy lab. Campus ministry could be a close group of five or six students gathered late on a weeknight for prayer and Holy Communion.

Here are other images of campus ministry servant leaders:

She's a first-semester student, new to the campus. She is isolated, lost, and agonizing over whether to quit and go home. She's asking for emotional support, but she also wants spiritual guidance.

He is a senior who still hasn't declared a major. He knows he's in trouble. But he's labored so long under his parents' expectations and his

Vicki Brown/GBHEM

Young people considering God's call to ordained ministry pray during EXPLORATION 2006 in Jacksonville, Fla.

professors' expectations and the expectations of his peers that he feels paralyzed, unable to make up his mind.

The professor stops by again today, "just to talk." His wife had died suddenly last semester, and he wonders how he can keep getting up every morning and going to class.

There has been racial tension on the campus for a week. On Friday, the

ExploreCalling.org Helps Examine Calling

ExploreCalling.org builds bridges between those exploring ministry as vocation and those who work as leaders or mentors in discernment and leadership development. The Web site invites people to consider God's call in their lives, provides answers to questions about candidacy and ministry in The United Methodist Church, and enables ongoing conversations that will "bridge" ministry candidates from one phase of vocational exploration to the next.

Developed by the General Board of Higher Education and Ministry, the Web site will help youth, college students, seminary students, and young adults who are considering how God is calling them and how they can serve in the UMC — either as lay people or as clergy.

Visitors to the site may sign up to receive updated information and highlighted features.

university president called asking for support in addressing the issue. Would the campus minister have any ideas about what to do next?

Creationism. Intelligent design. Evolution. The discussion at the university is generating lots of heat but little common ground. The vice president for academic affairs and the chair of the biosciences department decide to ask if the university chaplain would take a hand in sponsoring a campus-wide forum to focus the debate.

Two graduate students who knew you when they were undergrads ask if you'll officiate at their wedding. And another graduate calls to chat, say thanks for being with her through some difficult times, and report that things are going better now.

Ministry in higher education is demanding. It's also rewarding. Being a campus minister or a university chaplain demands a diversity of gifts, skills, education, commitments, and roles: preacher, teacher, negotiator, spiritual counselor, pastor, official college representative, public worship leader, small group convener, support for parents, adviser to university professors and administrators. It can be fast-paced, stressful, and demanding. But it is also stimulating, challenging, and deeply rewarding.

Campus ministers and university chaplains work with people ranging from 18-year-old high school graduates to 65-year-old faculty members and students. The campus minister's "congregation" may be racial-ethnic students and staff; second-career and returning women undergrads; science, law, and medical school students; fraternities and sororities; the custodial and maintenance staff.

Campus Ministry Issues and Opportunities

In addition to caring for people, those who minister in higher education also care about issues and institutions of learning: issues of values and education; what it means to be an educated person and a Christian; how faith and knowledge contribute to educating people to be citizens of their country and of the world. All of these are important facets of the work of a campus minister in higher education.

Some campus ministers and chaplains teach courses in religion and other disciplines; some teach courses for credit in the curriculum, while others teach non-credit course. Those who teach for credit often have completed, in addition to their theological degree, a doctorate (Ph.D., Ed.D., Th.D.) in the academic area.

Some teach in departments other than religion, such as philosophy, psychology, sociology, English, economics, or other areas. This means the individual is employed as a faculty member, meeting the same academic preparation requirements as other faculty. The annual conference may appoint an ordained clergyperson to teach at the institution. Likewise, ordained elders, ordained deacons, diaconal ministers, as well as other lay people may serve in administrative positions in the college or university, such as counselor, dean, or president.

Ministry in higher education engages mind and heart. It engages students and staff, faculty and administrators, the church and the world. It engages knowledge and vital piety. Writer Madeleine L'Engle sums up her experience in higher education in this way: "My own . . . college years were a mixture of joy and pain."* Joy and pain. And the campus minister is there for all of it. That is why campus ministry is so important, so challenging, and so unpredictable. It is good work. It is a good calling.

> *Orientation,* the award-winning magazine for graduating high school seniors and first-year college students, is now a Web resource. Visit www.gbhem.org/orientation to view a selection of both new articles and past favorites, prayers, and links to United Methodist loans and scholarships, programs, and events.

Reflection

- Think about unique gifts you may have to relate to young people who are making vocational decisions about their future.
- How may you be uniquely suited, or not, to work with college students, faculty and staff of all ages to help them grow in their faith development?

Mission Personnel

God calls all Christians to be in mission. Some are called to a particular mission witness and service through channels of ministry provided by the church.

General Board of Global Ministries

Global Ministries, the mission instrument of The United Methodist Church,

---

*Madeleine L'Engle, *Two-Part Invention: The Story of a Marriage* (San Francisco: Harper & Row, 1988).

is authorized to:

> *Recruit, send, and receive missionaries, enabling them to dedicate all or a portion of their lives in service across cultural, national, and political boundaries . . . and to facilitate the receiving and assignment of missionaries from churches in nations other than the United States in cooperation with the other general agencies and with annual conferences. (¶1302.3, 15, 2008 Book of Discipline)*

Other responsibilities of GBGM are numerous. A long list of duties described in ¶1302 *2008 Book of Discipline,* can be summarized around four goals:

- To make disciples of Jesus Christ
- To grow and strengthen congregations and their communities
- To alleviate human suffering
- To promote justice, peace, and freedom.

Mission Personnel Program Area

The GBGM Mission Personnel Program Area deals specifically with the identification, recruitment, selection, preparation, training, assignment, supervision, and support of mission personnel. It works with other units of the board in making decisions about personnel placements and assignments. Whenever possible, the placement of mission personnel is done in cooperation with United Methodist or other partner churches in the area of assignment.

The specific responsibilities of the Mission Personnel office are:

- To promote the opportunities for mission service related to Global Ministries throughout the constituencies of the Church.
- To recruit, select, prepare, and assign mission personnel, including, but not limited to, missionaries, deaconesses, US-2s, mission interns, and church and community workers.
- To provide all mission personnel with preparation and training for effective service in Global Ministries.
- To evaluate mission personnel for appropriate placement.
- To recommend persons as candidates for commissioning as deaconesses and missionaries, and to supervise and confirm the completion of all requirements for commissioning. (See pp. 47-48.)
- To engage in supervision and support of mission personnel through referral, transfer procedures, career counseling, missionary wellness, and personnel development, assisting them in the fulfillment of their missional vocation.
- To administer a diverse program of remuneration and benefits for personnel service.

- To offer training for mission service throughout the global church.
- To work with ecumenical agencies in fulfilling mission personnel responsibilities.
- To facilitate the receiving and assigning of missionaries–laity and clergy–from central conferences [outside the U.S.] and from autonomous, affiliated autonomous, and united churches, in cooperation with other boards and agencies and with annual conferences.
- To foster the support of mission personnel by congregations and individuals through Covenant Relationship Program, a feature of The Advance for Christ and His Church (See ¶821, *2008 Book of Discipline.*); and expand other forms of mission commitment including Global Mission Partners. (¶1313.6, *2008 Book of Discipline*)

Mission Service Types and Categories

There are three primary types of relationships between mission personnel and the General Board of Global Ministries.
- Commissioned personnel are missionaries, deaconesses, and others with whom the Church has established a covenant involving the "laying on of hands" for mission service.
- Non-commissioned personnel have not entered into a covenant but serve in a variety of capacities and locations.
- Persons in Mission (PIMs) are mission personnel of central conferences and partner churches outside the United States that the board helps to support.

Commissioned Personnel

Missionaries

Missionaries serve in a wide variety of ministries around the world, including the United States. They are assigned according to their gifts and abilities and mission needs at the time. Missionaries may be evangelists, pastors, doctors, nurses, teachers, agricultural specialists, youth workers, or social service providers. They may work in rural or urban settings; many serve women and children, and people who are poor, hungry, homeless, or otherwise pushed to the margins of societies.

United Methodist missionaries serve outside and within the United States; there are several U.S.-based groups of missionaries, including persons assigned to the Alaska and Red Bird (Kentucky) Missionary Conferences. The Church's National Plan for Hispanic and Latino Ministries incorporates a category of missionary service. These assignments are made in conjunction with annual conferences. The category of "home missionary" is no longer used for newly commissioned persons but there are individuals commissioned prior to 1988 who retain that designation.

Deaconesses and Home Missioners

Deaconesses, who are laywomen, and home missioners, who are lay-men, are professionally trained persons who have been led by the Holy Spirit to devote their lives to Christ-like service under the authority of the Church. They are approved by the General Board of Global Ministries (upon recommendation of the Mission Personnel Program Area) and commissioned by a bishop at a session of the (General Board of Global Ministries.) They shall have a continuing relationship to The United Methodist Church through the General Board of Global Ministries. (See ¶1314.2, 2008 Book of Discipline.)

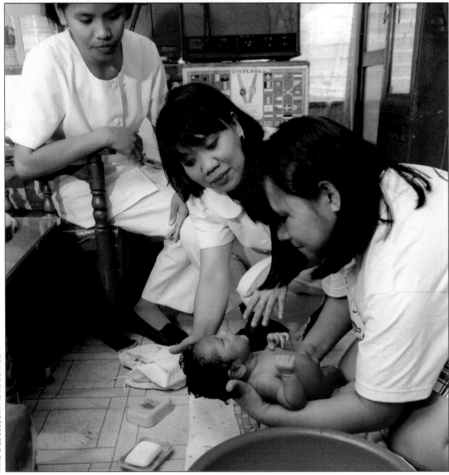

Mike DuBose/UM News Service

A public health nurse and a nurse-midwife instructor offer pointers to a new mother as she bathes her month-old son, during a home visit sponsored by Mary Johnston Hospital, Manila, Philippines.

Deaconesses and home missioners are available for service with any agency or program of The United Methodist Church. (They) may also serve in other than United Methodist Church agencies or programs provided that approval be given by the General Board of Global Ministries in consultation with the bishop of the receiving area. (¶1314.2, 2008 Book of Discipline)

Deaconesses and home missioners function through diverse forms of service directed toward the world to make Jesus Christ known in the fullness of his ministry and mission, which mandate that his followers:

- *Alleviate suffering.*
- *Erradicate the causes of injustice and all that robs life of dignity and worth.*
- *Facilitate the development of full human potential.*
- *Share in the building of the global community through the Church Universal. (¶1314.1, 2008 Book of Discipline)*

The Office of Deaconess was first authorized by the General Conference of The Methodist Episcopal Church in 1888 and was subsequently authorized in each of the predecessor organizations that now comprise The United Methodist Church. The relationship of home missioner was created by the General Conference of 2004 to recognize lay men who want to make a lifetime commitment to mission and the church.

Deaconesses and home missioners in active service hold membership in a local church within the annual conference where they are appointed to serve and are voting members of the charge conference of that church. Deaconesses and home missioners shall be seated at the sessions of the annual conference with voice and vote.

Church and Community Workers

The Church and Community Worker movement emerged more than a century ago to provide service and leadership development ministries in isolated rural areas. Today church and community workers work to uplift the poor and disenfranchised in rural and urban areas, primarily in the United States. Workers are assigned to cooperative parishes, ethnic ministries, criminal justice ministries, congregational health ministries, cooperative ministries, mission institutions, immigration services, and rural and urban ministries. Some are deaconesses. Both clergy and laity may serve in this mission category.

US-2 Missionaries

This more than 50-year old program provides two-year terms of mission service for young adults in the United States. Assignments are often to mission institutions, congregations, or projects engaged in community ministries, including community development, health services, youth ministries, education, and services for abused women and children. Objectives are to provide young adults with opportunities to explore church-related vocations and to provide leadership development opportunities.

Mission Interns

Mission Interns participate in a three-year cycle of service, 16 months outside the U.S. and 16 months inside the U.S. Their international assignments are most often in places of acute economic need; the U.S. portion may be spent in a mission institution, health and welfare agency, or in an urban ministry setting. Strong emphasis is placed on the development of a sense of global community and responsibility and on advocacy for peoples pushed aside by contemporary economic and social systems.

Non-Commissioned Personnel

The category of non-commissioned personnel covers groups and people with ties to the General Board of Global Ministries, but who are not in covenant relationships. They may be engaged in time-limited projects or provide support services. One group, community developers, operate from local bases but form a network that the board services.

Persons in Mission (PIMs) and International Persons in Mission (IPIMs)

These are mission personnel from partner churches outside the United States, serving in their own or another country.

Mission Volunteers

The United Methodist Church and its annual conferences in the U.S. offer a wide variety of volunteer mission opportunities for both teams and individuals. Volunteers are not considered mission personnel, and the church provides no compensation or benefits for them. However, volunteers perform extremely valuable mission services. Every annual conference has a volunteer service coordinator and the annual conferences work cooperatively with the General Board of Global Ministries through the Mission Volunteers Program Area.

Reflection

- Through Global Ministries, lay or ordained people (beginning as young adults) can respond to the call to mission service–in short-term service or lifetime commitment; in many different positions; and in many different locations. How would you describe this call as different from every Christian's call to servant ministry?

- What gifts, skills and interests could you bring to any of the multiple ways that one might be in mission service on behalf of the church either nationally or internationally?

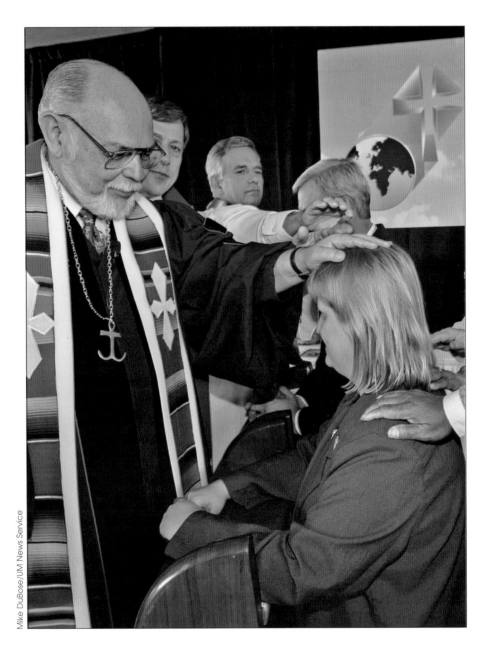

Chapter Three

Steps Into Servant Leadership

Steps Into Ministry for Young People

MAYBE YOU ARE EXPLORING HOW GOD WANTS YOU TO LIVE YOUR LIFE. YOU MAY BE beginning to think about vocational choices; or you may be experiencing a strong inclination toward a particular occupation or profession. You read in chapter one that coming to a place where God's intention for you and your gifts and talents match is a powerful indication of God's vocational call to you. Perhaps you do not feel any special calling, particularly to ordained ministry. However, you may be wondering what it might mean for you to respond as a baptized Christian to servant ministry.

The question is not whether you are called. The question is: How is God calling you to serve?

Those answering the call to ordained ministry are considered clergy. Servant leadership of other Christians is considered ministry of the laity.

Whether your vocation and career choice leads you to serve as a layperson or as an ordained person, listen to God's voice, seek wise counsel, do your own study and reflection, and follow the direction in which you are led.

- Talk with your youth minister, your church pastor or other church leader, your campus minister or chaplain.
- Meet with other young people and adults you respect who are engaged in a type of ministry that interests you.

EXPLORATION

Here's a chance to spend three days with other young people–high-school seniors through age 24–who are exploring ordained ministry. EXPLORATION is an informative and discerning weekend of worship, Bible study, prayer, workshops, and small group discussions. The event is held on a regular basis, as a national event in some years and by jurisdiction in other years. If you're wondering whether God might be calling you to ordained ministry, or if you want to find out what ministry in The United Methodist Church is all about, or would like some help sorting through the idea of Christian vocation, this gathering is for you. All baptized Christians are called to ministry. EXPLORATION may help you discover if your call might be to the ordained ministries of Word, Sacrament, Order, and Service in the church. For information, visit www.gbhem.org/exploration.

- Seek out honest feedback from people who know you well and can help you identify what your gifts and talents are.
- Read and reflect about the categories of service in this book.
- Explore the Web at sites like www.gbhem.org/exploration and www.IsGodCallingYou.org to find out about more about Christian vocation and how to answer God's call in your life.
- Above all, talk to God, listen to God, and wait for and respond to God's direction.

Mike DuBose/UM News Service

A young man lights candles to prepare the altar for Holy Communion Service.

Opportunities for Young People for Servant Leadership

- God does not wait for a certain age to call people into ordained ministry. If at an early age you feel this call, talk with your pastor about steps to explore the call. (See pp. 62-66, for Steps into Ordained Ministry.)
- If you find ministry with young people fascinating, there are opportunities, such as internships and shadow programs, that give you a chance to learn from others in children's ministry, youth ministry, or campus ministry. Talk to your youth pastor or other church leaders to see if these opportunities are available at your church.
- Churches often sponsor regional camps that hire college-age students to be on the ministry staff during the summer. Often these camps need counselors-in-training, as well, and hire older high school students for these positions. Contact your region's youth or camping ministry director to learn more.

Consider the following as you proceed to make a vocational choice:

Your Gifts–What spiritual gifts do you have to offer the church? What do you do well? What do enjoy? If you enjoy writing, offer to write a prayer for the congregation. If you are friendly and enjoy meeting people, offer to serve as a church greeter. If you are a good leader, volunteer to be an officer for your youth group. If you like to make speeches, consider training to become an official lay speaker. See the next section of this book for those steps. Whatever your gift, discover ways the church can use it. Ask your pastor about gifts discovery inventories to help discern your spiritual gifts.

The Division on Ministries with Young People provides a wealth of resources for youth, young adults, and those who work with young people. Visit the General Board of Discipleship Web site at www.gbod.org/youngpeople for information about events, grants, youth activities, articles by and about young people, and publications of interest to youth and young adults.

Your Passion–What really motivates you? Maybe you see a homeless person and want to make a change. Maybe you read about genocide in foreign countries and want to help stop it. Or maybe you're tired of hearing about people your age killing each other. How is the church responding? What ways can the church respond? How might you get involved or lead the movement yourself? Social justice ministries are important to the life of the church.

Your Daily Living–Think of ways you can incorporate what you know and learn from your faith into your daily living. You know you are empowered to live as Jesus lived. What does that mean in how you treat people at school? How does that shape your response to your family? Remember that the way you live is a ministry in itself.

Your Career Path–Maybe you are thinking of being a financial analyst, a doctor, a journalist, or a teacher. As you choose your career, think of ways you can serve God in what you do. You can also consider a career in the church. Churches sometimes need teachers for church schools. Conferences usually have communicators who write for newspapers and the Web about the church and deal with the media. Some congregations have parish nurses. Many churches need help with their finances. Think about how to shape your career as a service for God.

Your Devotional Life–Whatever ministry role you take, you must be prepared and fit for leadership. Taking Bible study courses and/or carving daily time for reading Scripture (even if just for five minutes) will better prepare you for your ministry.

Your Prayers–Be steadfast in prayer about what ways God can use you. Ask for guidance from God and be still to listen for God's direction. Ask others to pray for you as you discern what leadership you will take as a minister.

Steps Into Laity Leadership

The leadership of the laity has a long history in The United Methodist Church. While Methodist pastors rode the circuits, it was the leadership of the lay members of the societies that kept the congregational ministry going.

Beginning Steps

A good beginning step, if you feel you may be experiencing a call to serve, is to complete a spiritual gifts inventory. Study and reflect upon how your gifts, talents, and strengths, may be used in ministry, and/or in your daily life, community, and church. Take some time to consider your passion. What inspires you? What areas of mission or ministry excite you? What issues in the church or community bring you the deepest concern? When you use your spiritual gifts in conjunction with an area of ministry that you are passionate about wonderful things can and do happen.

Another step is critically important as you explore and prepare yourself for any form of ministry. Remain steadfast in the basic Christian practices or spiritual disciplines which John Wesley called means of grace. These means of grace include prayer, Bible study, the sacrament of Holy Communion, worship, fasting, and Christian conferencing. You may join or form a small group that will help you grow spiritually and stay faithful in your spiritual practices.

One group of this kind is a Covenant Discipleship Group. Small groups for support and accountability are a rich part of our Wesleyan heritage and continue today in many churches with a renewed vitality and relevance for growing in discipleship. Today's Covenant Discipleship Groups help their members witness to Jesus Christ in the world and follow his teachings through acts of compassion, justice, worship, and devotion under the guidance of the Holy Spirit. They focus on a balanced discipleship through works of piety (personal devotions and public worship), and works of mercy (acts of compassion and acts of justice).

Steps to Get Started with a Covenant Discipleship Group

- For your reading:
  - *Accountable Discipleship; Living in God's Household*, Steven W. Manskar, Discipleship Resources
  - *Guide for Covenant Discipleship Groups*, Gayle Turner Watson, Discipleship Resources
- Find a group of six to eight people who are interested in forming a Covenant Discipleship Group and encourage them to read the books so that they can understand the commitment involved.
- Go to www.gbod.org/smallgroup/cd to find more information on Covenant Discipleship Groups.

Opportunities and Steps for Servant Leadership

Class Leaders

Class leaders led the laity of the early Methodist church in developing their discipleship. Today, class leaders may be commissioned and classes may be organized to help form faithful disciples of Jesus Christ. Classes may organize as Bible studies or small groups.

If you feel called to use your gifts in this way:

- Assess your spiritual gifts. The gifts of teaching and leadership are helpful for this ministry role.
- Study the role of class leader by reading ¶1118.2, *2008 Book of Discipline*.
- Read *Class Leaders: Recovering a Tradition*, David Lowes Watson, Discipleship Resources.
- Develop a good working knowledge of the Bible through study books.
- Study United Methodist polity, tradition, and theology. Your pastor can refer you to reading resources.
- For more information on leading small groups go to www.gbod.org/smallgroup.

Ministry Area or Committee Chair

Leading within the congregation as part of a ministry team, committee member or committee chair is another form of servant ministry or servant leadership for lay people.

Resources to help you in this way:

- Participate in a spiritual gifts study to determine your spiritual gifts or complete a spiritual gifts assessment.
- Share the results of your spiritual gifts assessment with your pastor and/or the chair of the Lay Leadership Committee.
- Read a copy of the *Guidelines for Leading Your Congregation*, available from Cokesbury, for the area or committee of interest to you.
- Make your interest known to the pastor or nominating committee in your congregation so your name may be considered in this way.

Lay Member to Annual Conference

Lay members to annual conference have the responsibility to represent their congregation at annual conference and help interpret the actions and activities of the annual conference to their congregations.

To consider this servant leadership position:

- You must be a professing member of The United Methodist Church for

Mike DuBose/UM News Service

Missionary lay pastors in Cuba consecrate bicycles donated for their use by World Methodist Evangelism during a service at J.W. Branscomb Methodist Church.

two years and active in The United Methodist Church for four years. (See ¶¶32, 249, and 251.2, *2008 Book of Discipline*.)

- Lay members to annual conference are elected by the charge conference of your church.

Lay Leader

Lay leaders function as the primary representatives of the laity in the local church, district, or annual conference to which they are elected. The role of lay leader is not only to represent the laity, but also to support the pastor. In correlating positions, the district lay leader supports the district superintendent, while the conference lay leader supports the bishop. Laity in these roles can be prayer partners and share in mutual ministry with the clergy leaders.

Steps to take include:

- Assess your spiritual gifts. The gift of leadership is helpful for this role in the church.
- Lay leaders must be professing members of the local church and are elected by the charge conference of that church. (See ¶¶249 and 251, *2008 Book of Discipline*.)
- Read the *Lay Leader/Lay Member Guideline*, available from Cokesbury, to discover the responsibilities and considerations for the role of lay leader in the local church.
- It is a good option for lay leaders to consider becoming certified lay speakers.

Lay Speaker

Exhorters in the early Methodist societies challenged and encouraged the members in their spiritual growth. After a sermon by the pastor an exhorter would give practical applications of the sermon to the society members. The term *exhorter* has been replaced by *lay speaker* in today's UMC.

> *A lay speaker is a professing member of a local church or charge who is ready and desirous to serve the Church and who is well informed on and committed to the Scriptures and the doctrine, heritage, organization, and life of the United Methodist Church and who has received specific training to develop skills in witnessing to the Christian faith through spoken communication, church and community leadership, and care-giving ministries. (¶267,* 2008 Book of Discipline*)*

Lay speakers serve in their local church, or with additional training, serve beyond their local church in other churches, the district or the annual conference. Lay speaker training is not just about preaching. In fact, there are many more courses on other areas of ministry.

Training to become a lay speaker:

- Talk with your pastor regarding your interest in becoming a lay speaker. Lay speakers are recommended by their pastor and the church council or charge conference.
- Register for the Basic Course in Lay Speaking at either the district or conference level. Your pastor can help you get in touch with your district office to find information on classes. A list of Conference Directors of Lay Speaking Ministries may be found at www.gbod.org/laity under Lay Speaking.
- Read ¶267, *2008 Book of Discipline*.

The steps for becoming a certified lay speaker:

- Become a local church lay speaker.
- Take an advanced lay speaking course.
- Read ¶¶268-269, *2008 Book of Discipline*.

Lay Missioner

Lay missioners are committed lay persons, mostly volunteers, who are willing to be trained and work in a team with a pastor-mentor to develop faith communities, establish community ministries, develop church school extension programs, and engage in congregational development. All lay missioners must follow the guidelines established by the National Committee on Hispanic Ministries of the National Plan for Hispanic Ministries and may be certified by their annual conference. (¶270, 2008 Book of Discipline)

Lay missioners may be either Hispanic or non-Hispanic and must follow the guidelines found in the National Plan for Hispanic Ministry.

Steps to become a lay missioner:

- To be a lay missioner you must be an active participant in a local congregation of The United Methodist Church or the Methodist Church of Puerto Rico and demonstrate an appreciation for United Methodist doctrine and tradition as well as a knowledge of and commitment to the National Plan for Hispanic Ministries.
- Understand, appreciate, and affirm the existing Hispanic culture in the United States.
- Receive the recommendation of the pastor or appropriate committee of the local church in which you participate.
- Complete Modules I and II of the Training Program.

Certified Lay Minister

In order to enhance the quality of ministry to small membership churches, expand team ministry in churches and in deference to an expression of gifts and evidence of God's grace associated with the lay ministry of early Methodism, the certified lay minister is to be recognized and utilized. (See ¶271, 2008 Book of Discipline.)

Go to www.gbod.org/laity.clm to find more information.

Steps to Become a Certified Lay Minister:

- Become a certified lay speaker or complete equivalent training.
- Study ¶271, *2008 Book of Discipline.*
- Study and demonstrate an appreciation for UM history, polity, doctrine, worship, and liturgy through service in your local church.
- Receive the recommendation of your pastor and voted approval of the church council or charge conference.
- Complete the courses recommended by the General Board of Discipleship and the General Board of Higher Education and Ministry.
- Submit to appropriate screening for ministry.
- Receive the recommendation of the district superintendent.
- Apply in writing to the district committee on ordained ministry.
- Appear before the district committee on ordained ministry for review and approval.

Certified Professional Lay Ministry

Lay people serving in the church can enhance their learning and increase their knowledge and skills to become more effective workers in their areas of service. Certification in various areas of ministry within the church is available. These include Christian education, youth ministry, music, evangelism, camp/retreat ministry, spiritual formation, and older adult ministry. See page 77 for steps into certification for specialized ministry.

Leaders at any level set an example for others to follow. People will look to you as a leader, whether you are lay or clergy, for an example of how to live out their faith.

Commissioned Deaconess or Home Missioner

See page 75 for more information about this lifetime, full-time mission-oriented service.

Reflection

- List some ways that you are providing servant leadership now? What are some ways you can improve?

Steps Into Ordained Ministry

Those whom the Church ordains shall be conscious of God's call to ordained ministry, and their call shall be acknowledged and authenticated by the Church. . . . The Church cannot structure a single test of authenticity. Nevertheless, the experience of the Church and the needs of its ministry require certain qualities of faith, life, and practice from those who seek ordination as deacons and elders. (¶304, 2008 Book of Discipline)

Candidacy for ordained ministry is the first set of formal steps through which a person moves toward ordination and annual conference membership as a deacon or elder in full connection.

The Candidacy Process:

Step 1. The Inquiring Candidate
- Contact the pastor in a local church, another deacon or elder, or the district superintendent to inquire about the candidacy process.
- Reading of *The Christian as Minister* is recommended.
- Use of *Understanding God's Call: A Ministry Inquiry Process* is recommended or may be required by the annual conference board of ordained ministry. (This resource is available from Cokesbury.)

Step 2. Application and Enrollment
- Apply to the district superintendent in writing for admission to the candidacy program and to be assigned a candidacy mentor by the district committee in consultation with the district superintendent.
- Applicant must have been a member of The United Methodist Church for at least one year or a baptized participant of a recognized United Methodist campus ministry or other United Methodist ministry setting.
- After online candidacy enrollment with GBHEM and payment of the application fee, the candidate will study the resources adopted by the conference board of ordained ministry. The *Guidelines for Candidacy* manual is recommended.

Step 3. Public Declaration of Candidacy
- Consult with the pastor and pastor/staff parish relations committee, or equivalent body specified by the district committee on ordained ministry sharing a written statement reflecting on the call, written responses to disciplinary questions, and requesting recommendation as a certified candidate. Graduation from an accredited high school or a certificate of equivalency is required.

- The charge conference of the local church or equivalent body will then make a recommendation to the district committee on ordained ministry.

Step 4. Certified Candidacy

- Appear before the district committee for examination and approval as a certified candidate.

Courtesy of Drew University, The Theological School

Students chat outside Seminary Hall at The Theological School at Drew University in Madison, N.J.

- To meet the committee, you must complete psychological assessment as required by the annual conference.
- Submit a written response to questions found in ¶311.2a, *2008 Book of Discipline*.
- Agree to maintain the highest ideals of Christian life as set forth in ¶¶102-104; ¶¶160-166, *2008 Book of Discipline*.

Step 5. Licensed Local Pastor Studies (Optional)
- A certified candidate may apply for license as a local pastor after completing studies prescribed by the General Board of Higher Education and Ministry and administered by the conference board of ordained ministry, or after completing one-third of the work for a master of divinity degree.
- Licensing studies are a prerequisite to appointment as a full-time, part-time, or student local pastor.
- A local pastor must make satisfactory progress in the Course of Study.

(See ¶¶315-316, *2008 Book of Discipline*, for a fuller understanding of the ministry of licensed local pastor. Local pastors may be elected to associate membership upon recommendation of the board of ordained ministry. Go to page 66 for more detail.)

Step 6. Candidacy Renewal
- Progress is reviewed through an annual interview and candidacy renewed annually by the district committee on ordained ministry, following recommendation by the charge conference.

Step 7. Completion of Candidacy toward Provisional Membership
- Candidacy Requirement: Candidate shall have been a certified candidate for at least one year and no more than 12.
- Service Requirement: Candidate shall have demonstrated his or her gifts for ministries of service and leadership to the satisfaction of the district committee on ordained ministry.
- Undergraduate Requirement: Candidate shall have completed a bachelor's degree from a United Methodist University Senate approved school. Exceptions may be made. (See ¶324.3, *2008 Book of Discipline*.)
- Graduate Requirement:
  - Candidates for both deacon and elder shall have completed one-half of a minimum of 24 semester hours of basic graduate theological studies (BGTS) in the areas of Old Testament, New Testament, theology, church history, mission, worship/liturgy, evangelism, and United Methodist doctrine, polity, and history.

- Candidate for elder shall have completed one-half of the studies toward a Master of Divinity or its equivalent including one-half of the BGTS from a seminary listed by the University Senate.
  - Candidate for deacon shall have completed one-half of the studies of a master's degree from a University Senate-approved school, or received a master's degree in the area of ministry in which one will serve and completed one-half of the BGTS.
- Alternate Routes to Ordination:
  - See ¶324.5, *2008 Book of Discipline*, for alternate route for deacons.
  - See ¶324.6, *2008 Book of Discipline*, for alternate route for local pastors.
- Other Requirements: Candidate shall a) present a satisfactory certificate of health; b) respond to a written and oral doctrinal examination; c) provide a written concise autobiographical statement; d) be interviewed and recommended by the district committee; e) submit a form provided by the conference board of ordained ministry with a notarized statement detailing any written accusations or convictions for felony, misdemeanor, or incident of sexual misconduct or child abuse; and f) have a personal interview with the conference board of ordained ministry.

Step 8 Full Membership and Ordination as a Deacon or Elder

- Candidates who have been provisional members for at least two full annual conference years following completion of educational requirements may be admitted into membership in full connection in the annual conference and ordained as a deacon or an elder.
- Deacon candidates are required to a) serve under episcopal appointment in a ministry of service, supervised by a district superintendent and the conference board of ordained ministry; and b) respond to an examination administered by the conference board on the covenantal relationship to God, the church, and the Order of Deacon, the understanding of *diaconia*, servant leadership, and the interrelatedness of the church and the world.
- Elder candidates are required to a) serve full time under episcopal appointment, supervised by a district superintendent and the conference board; b) prepare a sermon on a passage specified by the conference board and present a plan for teaching a book of the Bible; and c) respond to an examination administered by the conference board in the areas of theology and vocation.
- Other requirements for ordination for both deacon and elder may be put in place by each conference board of ordained ministry.

Associate Members (Optional)

Licensed local pastors may be recommended to associate membership by the conference board of ordained ministry when they have met the following conditions:

- reached age 40
- served four years as full-time local pastors
- completed the five-year Course of Study, in addition to studies for licensing
- completed a minimum of 60 semester hours toward a bachelor of arts or equivalent in a University Senate-approved school
- prepared at least one written sermon on a biblical passage specified by the conference board and given satisfactory answers in a written doctrinal examination (considering questions listed in ¶324.9, *2008 Book of Discipline*)

(See ¶¶321-322, *2008 Book of Discipline*, for a fuller understanding of the ministry of associate members.)

For further information contact:

Division of Ordained Ministry
General Board of Higher Education and Ministry
PO Box 340007
Nashville, TN 37203-0007
615-340-7389
E-mail: dom@gbhem.org
Web site: www.gbhem.org/ministry

Young Adult Seminarians Network

Young Adult Seminarians Network (YASN) is a network of United Methodist seminarians ages 35 and younger. The network began in 2004, when 26 young seminarians representing 17 seminaries met to envision and create the network.

YASN is dedicated to: helping members grow in the faith, to deepen their relationship with Jesus Christ, to support each other in the faith journey, to be advocates for social justice, and to take an active role in The United Methodist Church.

Resources for spiritual formation, models for sabbath retreats, suggestions for navigating the ordained ministry candidacy process, and pointers for relating to boards of ordained ministry are YASN's emphases.

Visit their Web site and contact them at www.yasn.org.

Steps to Become Endorsed

Endorsement is the credential which certifies that a clergyperson performs a valid ministry of The United Methodist Church and has presented evidence of required specialized education, training, skills and, when required, professional certification necessary to perform that ministry. Once that clergyperson no longer serves in that particular setting, the endorsement is withdrawn (¶1421.5c(3), 2008 Book of Discipline)

Who Needs Endorsement?

The *Book of Discipline* states that the United Methodist Endorsing Agency has responsibility for people appointed to ministries of pastoral care in specialized settings including, but not limited to, ministry in the military, correctional institutions, the Department of Veterans Affairs, healthcare settings, pastoral counseling, marriage and family counseling, workplace ministries, community service ministries, and other related ministry settings that conference boards of ordained ministry and bishops may designate. Clergy to be appointed to any of the above extension ministry appointments shall receive ecclesiastical endorsement.

What is Ecclesiastical Endorsement?

Ecclesiastical endorsement is an affirmation that a person is, or will be, performing a valid extension ministry consistent with the covenantal community of The United Methodist Church and has presented evidence of having the special education, experience, and skills necessary to perform that ministry. Endorsement is given to a specific setting. Should an individual move from one setting to another, the endorsement will be reviewed and, if approved, issued to the new setting. From application to endorsement, the process normally takes two to four months.

Requirements for Ecclesiastical Endorsement

People seeking ecclesiastical endorsement to a specific setting must meet the following criteria:

- deacon, elder, provisional member, or associate member of an annual conference
- graduation from an accredited college and seminary
- additional requirements as specified by the setting

Requirements for Associate Status

Licensed local pastors who desire to serve in a ministry in a specialized setting may apply to the United Methodist Endorsing Agency for associate status.

The Endorsement Process

- Contact the United Methodist Endorsing Agency (UMEA) via mail, phone, or e-mail to receive an application.
- Applicants are responsible for providing materials requested on the application form to UMEA.
- Provide names and addresses of two personal references and your district superintendent.
- Provide a life sketch and statement of ministry.
- Complete the interview process.

The Interview

- A central interviewing committee is made up of endorsed chaplains. Whenever possible, at least one member of the committee will represent the setting for which you seek endorsement.
- The purpose of this interview is to understand your perception of Christian faith as it relates to the setting in which you desire to minister.
- One member of the committee will serve as presenter for you and will be especially familiar with your materials in detail. You will be notified of the recommendation at the time of your interview.
- Following the interview, the committee will make a recommendation to the endorsing committee.
- The endorsing committee has the authority to grant or deny ecclesiastical endorsement. It is composed of members elected to the General Board of Higher Education and Ministry (GBHEM) Board of Directors. The committee meets three times a year and has responsibility for policy and process regarding endorsement. Endorsement is valid only while you are under appointment to the setting for which endorsement was granted.

Change of Endorsed Settings

Contact UMEA if you change settings, a new endorsement may be required. (¶1421.5, *2008 Book of Discipline*) Endorsement for chaplaincy does not guarantee employment or appointment. Employers establish criteria that the church does not influence. For example, maximum age limits for initial entry, physical fitness, and security clearances are three requirements that are set by the military departments. The Federal Bureau of Prisons has similar requirements. Other endorsements often require experience in the specialized setting and documentation as to effectiveness in that ministry. Others may require membership in a pastoral care organization.

Endorsement for Deacons

There are four components of service as a chaplain: appointment, endorsement, certification, and employment. A deacon may be appointed to serve as a chaplain if the request for appointment is approved by the bishop; if endorsement is granted; if the deacon is working toward certification; and, if an employer is willing to hire.

It is critical to understand that deacons have no sacramental authority, and therefore, may not be eligible for all settings requiring endorsement. Deacons are eligible for endorsement to non-military settings and must meet the same requirements as elders: provisional or full conference membership, training, experience, and certification as appropriate. Endorsement to military settings is limited to elders due to the requirement for sacramental authority in those settings.

Civilian Chaplaincy

Standards for endorsement include relationship with and/or certification by the appropriate national professional pastoral care organization.

Those recognized include:

- American Association for Marriage and Family Therapy (AAMFT) www.aamft.org

Mike DuBose/UM News Service

United Methodist Chaplain Ernest P. Jay West blends the roles of pastor and soldier while serving with the U.S. Army's 101st Airborne Division (Air Assault) at Fort Campbell, Ky.

- American Association on Intellectual and Developmental Disibilities (AAIDD) www.aaidd.org
- American Association of Pastoral Counselors (AAPC) www.aapc.org
- American Correctional Chaplains Association (ACCA) www.correctional chaplains.org
- Association for Clinical Pastoral Education (ACPE) www.acpe.edu
- Association of Professional Chaplains (APC) www.professional chaplains.org
- College of Pastoral Supervision and Psychotherapy (CPSP) www.cpsp.org
- Federation of Fire Chaplains (FFC) www.firechaplains.org
- International Conference of Police Chaplains (ICPC) www.icpc4cops.org
- National Institute of Business & Industrial Chaplaincy (NIBIC) www.nibic.com
- National Association of Veterans Affairs Chaplains (NAVAC) www.navac.net
- Contact information is also available at the UMEA Web site: www.gbhem.org/chaplains, or by calling 615-340-7411, or e-mail: umea@gbhem.org.

In situations not covered by recognized certifying agencies, GBHEM will set minimum standards which may include specialized training for the type of ministry for which endorsement is sought and may include at least one year of supervised clinical training or comparable professional experience.

Civilian Endorsement Settings

1. Children's Home
2. Clinical Pastoral Education
3. General Hospital
4. Hospice
5. Marriage and Family Therapy
6. Mental Health
7. Mental Retardation
8. Pastoral Counseling
9. Police
10. Prison/Correctional Institution
11. Retirement Community
12. Specialized
13. Substance Abuse
14. Veterans Affairs
15. Workplace

Military Chaplaincy

Army: Active, Reserve, National Guard

Navy: Active, Reserve

Air Force: Active, Reserve, Air National Guard

Basic requirements for initial appointment to active duty or reserve:

- be a citizen of the United States
- be physically qualified for general service based on an examination by the military
- meet current requirements determined by the military

Applicants are responsible for contacting the military branch for which they are seeking endorsement.

For military branch contact information, go to:

- www.gbhem.org/chaplains
- umea@gbhem.org
- 615-340-7411

Steps Into Mission Service

Candidates for mission service through The United Methodist Church should develop relations with both the Mission Personnel Program Area of Global Ministries and with the conference committee on mission personnel of their annual conference.

The contact for the denominational mission personnel office is:

Mission Personnel

General Board of Global Ministries

475 Riverside Drive, Room 320

New York, NY 10115

Telephone: 212-870-3660

Fax: 212-870-3774

http://new.gbgm-umc.org/about/us/mp/about/

A frequently updated list of the chairpersons of conference committees on mission personnel can be found on the internet at http://new.gbgm-umc.org/about/us/mp/documents/ccmpaddresses. However, not all conferences currently have such a committee. Should a conference not have this committee, a candidate should contact the conference secretary of global ministries (names at same web site) and also directly approach the Mission Personnel Office of the General Board of Global Ministries."

Candidates submit applications (see below) and undergo a series of screenings. If they are selected, they take part in training appropriate to their expected assignment and the nature of the work they will assume.

Qualifications for Service

While the general qualifications are similar, some differences exist in the specific qualifications and procedures for missionaries and for deaconess/ home missioner. These differences are reflected below.

The qualifications for missionaries are as follows:

- Faith Confession: All people assigned as General Board of Global Ministries mission personnel must be Christians. Although membership in The United Methodist Church or other Methodist Churches is not required for missionaries, it is recommended. Deaconesses and home missioners must be members of The United Methodist Church since they are members of the annual conferences in which they actively serve. Familiarity with and commitment to the United Methodist *Discipline*, that is, its polity and its structures, are required.
- Church Experience: Leadership experience and mission service through congregations and annual conferences is desirable.
- Clergy and Laity: Lay people as well as clergy can be assigned to mission service. Seminary training is necessary only when assigned as a pastor or seminary professor. Those assigned as pastors must be ordained clergy and be in good standing with an annual conference.
- Assignments: All of the General Board of Global Ministries missionaries are assigned to locations where there are defined mission needs and where personnel are requested by local mission partners (Central Conferences, partner autonomous Methodist or united Churches). Missionaries do not initiate, create, nor design their own assignments. Deaconesses and home missioners may serve in church related vocations or helping professions.
- Terms: Different programs require different lengths of service. Missionary assignments do not require a lifetime commitment, although long-term commitments are encouraged and anticipated. Missionaries typically serve three-year, renewable terms.
- Education Requirements: A bachelor's degree is required as a minimum. However, educational requirements vary with each mission service category. If an applicant does not have an academic resume, necessary equivalent vocational and/or life experience can be considered.
- Professional Credentials: All professionals (clergy, physicians, educators) must have the appropriate credentials/licenses for their field in order to be commissioned as mission personnel.
- Experience with Diversity: Experience working with and serving people of different racial-ethnic, socio-economic, and cultural backgrounds are advisable.

- Language: Fluency in a language or languages other than English is an asset although not a requirement for application. Language study may be required for a particular assignment.

Required Application Information and Procedure for Missionaries

The following are required:

- Mission Personnel Information Form and Skills and Professional Experience Sheet. (Up-to-date application forms and information are available on the internet at http://new.gbgm-umc.org/about/us/mp/documents.)
- Academic Transcripts. Transcripts are required from each institution of higher education that has awarded a degree. They must bear the signature and seal of the school. Transcripts should not be opened when received by mission service applicants; rather, they should remain in the sealed envelope for transmittal with the application.
- References. Six people should serve as references. They should first be contacted for permission to list them. Once permission is received, a candidate places his or her name on the Reference Form and sends the form to each reference along with a self-addressed, stamped envelope. References will return the completed forms to candidates with their signatures affixed across the sealed flap of the envelope. Candidates do not open these letters but retain them sealed for submission.

Submission of Documents

Mail the personnel information form, the transcripts, and the letters of reference to the chair of the conference committee on mission personnel or, in the absence of such a committee, to Global Ministries Mission Personnel Program Area. If in doubt about where to send documents, contact the Mission Personnel Program Area of the General Board of Global Ministries.

Favorable review of application leads to an interview with the conference committee on mission personnel. Approved applicants engage in further interviews, psychological evaluation, medical clearance, and training.

Personnel Information Form

This form requests information on name, address, family, church relationship, educational background, work experience, special skills, and area of mission interest. Current versions of the form can be obtained online or by contacting the Mission Personnel Program Area. It also requests concise responses to questions under four headings, as follows:

1. Christian Experience
   - In what ways do you experience the presence of God in your life?
   - Describe the discipline you follow in your prayer life.

- What do you believe about the Bible?
- Describe ways in which you have been able to share your faith with others and lead them to believe in Jesus.

2. Understanding of Mission
   - How do you understand the nature and mission of the Church?
   - What influences have helped shape your understanding?
   - How have you been involved in the mission of the Church?
   - What factors have drawn you to pursue a vocation in mission service? Which factors have been most important?

3. Personal Relationships and Interpersonal Skills
   - How have you prepared for participation in mission service?
   - Why do you believe God is leading you to mission service?
   - Describe your strengths.
   - Describe your weaknesses.
   - What has been your experience of your working relationship with supervisors?

4. Professional Competence and Educational Preparation
   - Where do you believe you are called to serve, and in what capacity?
   - What continuing education activities have you participated in during the past three years?

Paul Jeffery/UM News Service

Tammi Mott, a United Methodist from Unadilla, N.Y., helps rebuild a home, in the West Bank town of Anata, that the Israeli military has demolished four times. Mott works for ACT member Church World Service.

- List some titles and authors of books you have read in the past year.
- List newspapers and periodicals that you read regularly.
- Which historical person do you most admire? Why?

Qualifications for Becoming a Deaconess and Home Missioner

- A call from God to lifetime, full-time, mission-oriented service
- Membership in The United Methodist Church
- The basic qualifications for the ministry to which one is called (i.e., education, training, professional certifications, life experiences, etc.)
- Ability to work with people from all racial/ethnic and socioeconomic backgrounds
- Employment in a church-related vocation or helping profession
- Continuation of the practice of discernment
- Biblical/theological grounding in the following studies:
  - Old Testament
  - New Testament
  - Theology of Mission
  - History of The United Methodist Church
  - Polity and Doctrine of The United Methodist Church
- Commitment to functioning through diverse forms of service directed toward the world to make Jesus Christ known in the fullness of his ministry and mission which mandates that his followers:
  - alleviate suffering
  - eradicate causes of injustice and all that robs life of dignity and worth
  - facilitate the development of full human potential
  - share in building global community through the church universal.

Required Application Information and Procedure for Deaconesses and Home Missioners

- Applicant completes and returns to the Deaconess Program Office the Mission Personnel Information Form (application including reference forms) with copy to the chairperson of the committee on mission personnel in the annual conference for review and recommendation.
- Personnel Information Form is circulated to and reviewed by members of the Personnel Services Staff Team.
- Letter is sent to applicant regarding the action of Mission Personnel.
- Approved applicant invited for staff interview and psychological interview/testing (generally in New York) and participation in the theology of mission course.
- Letter sent to the applicant regarding the final action of Mission Personnel Program Area.

- Approved applicant moves to the candidate stage and begins or completes core studies requirements (Old Testament, New Testament, theology of mission, history of The United Methodist Church, polity and doctrine of The United Methodist Church.)
- Upon completion of core studies requirement, or if registered for remaining core studies class(es), candidate is invited to participate in the next scheduled orientation/preparation/ training.
- Confirmation is requested of candidate's full-time (at least 21 hours or more per week) employment in a church-related vocation or helping profession.
- Candidate is commissioned to the Office of Deaconess by a bishop at a meeting of the Board of Directors of the General Board of Global Ministries.

Commissioning

The act of commissioning is an outward and visible sign that recognizes an inward experience. Through it, the church acknowledges and authenticates the ministry of mission personnel by the laying on of hands. This act signifies that those commissioned are sent into the world on behalf of and under the authority of the church, as representatives of Christ's love and concern.

Commissioning takes place after a candidate is accepted and, usually, after a period of training. This is a public event to which the family and friends of candidates are invited. It is a time of commitment and celebration.

Commissioning recognizes that people are called by God to participate in God's mission. This calling is grounded in an understanding of Christian baptism as the call to every Christian to involvement in mission and ministry. Commissioning recognizes a vocational call to a mission task under the *Discipline* of The United Methodist Church. It signifies that a person has satisfactorily completed the qualifying process and training as stipulated by the General Board of Global Ministries. Commissioning establishes a covenant. The parties are God, the individual, and the family of faith in the church.

In receiving the commission, mission personnel pledge to:
- Proclaim Christ to the world and exemplify God's grace, peace, and justice.
- Continue to grow in grace and to embrace God's mission as found in global, ecumenical, and interreligious expressions.
- Interpret mission as practiced by The United Methodist Church through the General Board of Global Ministries, supporting denominational and board policy, practice, structure, and linkages.
- Accept and embody a simple lifestyle that may not include compensation or benefits levels found in secular employment.
- Cooperate with the ecumenical community.

Commissioning signifies that mission personnel will receive from the General Board of Global Ministries and The United Methodist Church:

- Support through prayer
- Mission assignments or opportunities (as defined in service categories)
- Appropriate ongoing preparation and training
- Spiritual, financial, and caring support.

The qualifications for commissioning include:

- Christian commitment and an understanding of the mission calling
- Completion of the application and training process
- Intercultural/ethnic/racial experience and understanding
- Skills in interpersonal relations and leadership development
- Appropriate educational and professional qualifications
- Physical and emotional health
- The willingness to enter into a covenant with The United Methodist Church through the General Board of Global Ministries.

Steps Into Certification in Areas of Specialized Ministry

Certification in Christian education, youth ministry, music ministry, evangelism, camp and retreat ministry, older adult ministry, and spiritual formation by The United Methodist Church resulted from a desire of people in these fields to serve the church with excellence. It is available to qualifying lay people, deacons, elders, local pastors and diaconal ministers.

Certification is the church's recognition that an individual has met the required standards for academic training, experience, and continuing study necessary to achieve and maintain professional excellence in areas of specialized ministry.

The church's need for individuals who can serve to the best of their ability makes certification by The United Methodist Church increasingly important.

Graduate Certification

Certification is available to those who have completed a graduate degree in an area of specialization that includes approved core courses and to those who have an undergraduate degree and complete the core graduate courses for their specialized area. In both cases the courses must be taken at an institution approved by the General Board of Higher Education and Ministry (GBHEM).

Step 1

Make interest known to the certification registrar of the annual conference board of ordained ministry.

Step 2

Obtain and study the leaflet outlining the professional certification standards and personal, church, academic, and professional requirements in the area of specialized ministry desired and complete enrollment form #HE4064. An annual conference may require approval of the person before enrollment is complete. Send to the annual conference certification registrar and a copy to:

General Board of Higher Education and Ministry
Division of Ordained Ministry, Education Team
PO Box 340007
Nashville, TN 37203-0007

Enrollment forms can be obtained from the annual conference registrar or downloaded from the General Board of Higher Education and Ministry Web site: www.gbhem.org/certification.

Step 3: Personal Requirements

- Recognized Christian character, personal competence, integrity, and commitment to the church's total ministry and mission.
- Ability to function with emotional maturity and sound judgment, ability to relate to people, and to work with volunteers and staff.
- Demonstrated leadership, ability to integrate theory and practice, understanding of the commitment to the educational ministry of the church.

Step 4: Church Requirements

- A member of The United Methodist Church for at least two years immediately prior to enrollment in the process.
- Knowledge of The United Methodist Church's structure, polity, curriculum resources, program, and mission.

Step 5: Academic Requirements

Applicants must meet the educational standards set by the Division of Ordained Ministry, Education Team, General Board of Higher Education and Ministry, The United Methodist Church. It is important to carefully study the appropriate leaflet. (See Step 2.)

For information on dates and locations of certification courses currently being offered check the General Board of Higher Education and Ministry Web site: www.gbhem.org/certification.

To be eligible for financial assistance from the General Board of Higher Education and Ministry, enrollment forms must be received by GBHEM prior to registering for the first course.

Step 6: Professional Requirements

People must have two years of experience in the area of their respective discipline. This experience can be gained through two years in a full-time job/appointment with The United Methodist Church or four years of part-time employment. People must be serving at the time they seek certification.

Step 7

Following the required experience for the certification being sought, and when all academic requirements have been met, individuals may apply for professional certification using the application form 323790. Applicants can obtain the form from their annual conference board of ordained ministry or download it from www.gbhem.org/certification.

Step 8

Each applicant must submit a minimum of three references from persons acquainted with his/her personal, church, and professional qualifications.

The three references must include a United Methodist ordained elder or ordained deacon in full connection, a college or seminary professor under whom the individual has studied, and a general officer in a local church with whom the person seeking certification has worked.

Applicants must send the completed application form and all transcripts to the annual conference board of ordained ministry and a copy to the Division of Ordained Ministry, Education Team, GBHEM, PO Box 340007, Nashville, TN 37203-0007.

Step 9

The annual conference board of ordained ministry will conduct a background check of the applicant and make arrangements for them to receive psychological testing.

Step 10

The Division of Ordained Ministry, Education Team, will review the application to determine that all academic and professional requirements have been met and notify the annual conference board of ordained ministry. The board will then interview the applicant to determine if all standards and requirements for professional certification are met and make the decision to grant professional certification.

Step 11

Upon vote by the conference board of ordained ministry indicating the applicant has satisfactorily met all requirements for certification, the board will notify the Division of Ordained Ministry that the application is approved. After satisfactory review by the division, the certificate will be prepared and sent to the conference board of ordained ministry.

Step 12
The conference board of ordained ministry will present the certificate to the individual, usually at a session of the annual conference.

Step 13
Professional certification is subject to biennial review and approval by the conference board of ordained ministry. The individual must continue to meet the standards maintained by the Division of Ordained Ministry. Every other year the conference board will send all certified persons the renewal form which must be completed and returned by the date specified. Certification is renewable for as long as the certified person desires it, contingent upon satisfactory completion of the biennial renewal form which includes an active program of continuing education and approval of the conference BOM.

Undergraduate Certification
Certification is available to graduates from an undergraduate institution with a major in a specialized ministry area when the institution's program has been approved by the General Board of Higher Education and Ministry. For a list of these institutions, see the GBHEM Web site at www.gbhem.org/certification. After graduation these people must serve two years in their specialized ministry area before applying for certification. The process for certification outlined in the steps on the immediate previous pages should be followed omitting Steps 2 and 5.

Paraprofessional Certification
Paraprofessional certification is available to those working in areas of specialized ministry through programs approved by the General Board of Higher Education and Ministry. These programs are available through some jurisdictions, annual conferences, colleges, and seminaries. Paraprofessional certification does not have academic credit and is designed for people who are at least 35 years old and who have not had the opportunity to complete an undergraduate degree, and are seeking training in a specialized ministry. Those seeking paraprofessional certification should complete the following steps.

Step 1
Same as Graduate Certification requirement, page 77.

Step 2

Obtain and study the leaflet outlining the requirements for paraprofessional certification including required course work. Register with the program chosen to fulfill the course requirements. Program information can be obtained from the annual conference or at the GBHEM Web site: www.gbhem.org/certification.

Step 3 Personal Requirements

Same as Graduate Certification requirement, page 78.

Step 4 Church Requirements

Same as Graduate Certification requirement, page 78.

Step 5 Course Requirements

Applicants must have completed a course of work approved by the GBHEM Division of Ordained Ministry Education Team. (Information on approved programs can be obtained from the conference office or at the GBHEM Web site: www.gbhem.org/certification.)

Step 6 Experience in Area of Specialized Ministry

Anyone seeking paraprofessional certification must have two years' experience in their area of specialized ministry at the time of applying for certification. This can be through part-time or full-time employment or volunteering in a United Methodist Church setting.

Step 7

Following the meeting of requirements individuals may apply for paraprofessional certification by completing an application form available from the annual conference registrar or GBHEM at the contact information listed above.

Step 8

Each applicant must submit a minimum of three references from someone acquainted with her/his personal standards, church relationship, and course work. The three must include a United Methodist ordained deacon or elder, a course work teacher under whom the person has studied, and a general officer in a local church with whom the person seeking certification has worked.

Step 9

The completed application form must be sent to the registrar of the annual conference board of ordained ministry and a copy to:

Division of Ordained Ministry, Education Team
General Board of Higher Education and Ministry
PO Box 340007
Nashville, TN 37203-0007

Libba Gillum

Chaplains and pastoral counselors provide counseling and support in many settings including hospitals, nursing homes, prisons, and the workplace. They are endorsed for service in a particular setting.

Step 10

The board of ordained ministry will conduct a background check of the applicant. A psychological background test may also be required.

Step 11

The Division of Ordained Ministry Education Team will review the application to determine that all requirements have been met and notify the annual conference board of ordained ministry. The board will then interview the applicant and if all standards and requirements have been met make a decision to grant para-professional certification.

Step 12

Upon vote of the conference board of ordained ministry indicating the applicant has been approved for certification the Division of Ordained ministry Education Team will be notified and prepare the certificate and send it to the board of ordained ministry who will present it to the applicant, usually at the annual conference session.

Step 13

Renewal same as Graduate Certification requirement, page 80.

Chapter Four

Guidelines for Using the Text

AS A DEACON, ELDER, LOCAL PASTOR, CHAPLAIN, CAMPUS MINISTER, OR OTHER CLERGY OF The United Methodist Church, one of the most significant and satisfying tasks you have is to help identify, advise, and assist those called to servant leadership in our denomination. For many, this responsibility is not so much a task as it is the joy and satisfaction of relating to people and their deepest level of need at the time of a major vocational decision.

You can assist people exploring vocational options in many ways.

- You can direct them to this text, a vocational guide for service opportunities in The United Methodist Church.
- You can meet with them and use *The Christian as Minister* and *Understanding God's Call: A Ministry Inquiry Process* as the basis of a series of conversations on the meaning of Christian vocation.
- You can help them see beyond the seemingly impersonal, formal requirements for ministry in The United Methodist Church to the intention of the church to find the most effective people for its leadership.
- You may have opportunities to help inquiring people examine a variety of leadership possibilities, receive feedback on their leadership potential, and test their leadership skills.
- You may also have insights about their family and background that will

be helpful to the individuals or to the committees that may consider them for ministerial service.

If you know of serious factors that may mean the individual should not be encouraged further in the exploration of a particular form of ministry, it is important that you discuss these with the individual. Regardless of the outcome of the inquiry, your concern is equally for the inquirer and the future leadership needs of the church.

Using *The Christian as Minister* as a Guide with Others

The Christian as Minister was written to assist you in vocational guidance work with others. In using this resource, the following guidelines may be helpful:

- Carefully read through *The Christian as Minister* and participate in any training offered through the district committee or conference board of ordained ministry.
- As you become familiar with the contents, you will see various ways it can be used in the interpretation of God's call to ministry. You may also discover new information about the options for ministerial service, their standards and requirements.
- The more thoroughly you know the contents of this vocational text, the better equipped you will be to inform others and counsel those who sense a call to servant ministry or servant leadership.

Suggested Uses by Clergy

- Order a supply of *The Christian as Minister* for your study, church library, office, or workplace.
- Use sections of *The Christian as Minister* with your pastor/staff parish relations committee, confirmation class, or any other group that wishes to study the meaning of Christian vocation.
- Give a copy to those you believe are considering a church-related occupation. Ask them to study the book carefully and note any questions or insight gained.

Use *The Christian as Minister* as a study guide with the Pastor/Staff Parish Relations Committee

- Help the committee to gain insight into a theology of ministry.
- Review the committee's responsibility for interviewing and recommending candidates for ordained and licensed ministry to the charge conference.
- Clarify the steps a candidate must take in order to enter ordained or licensed ministry.
- Discuss the resources the church can provide to assist a person who wishes to enter a church-related occupation.

- Identify other resources available through the district, conference, or general agencies of the church that can assist as well.

Offer to counsel with those inquiring into church-related occupations

- Explore the meaning of God's mission, Christ's call to servant leadership, an understanding of vocation, and the options for ministry in The United Methodist Church.
- Help the inquirers to see themselves as others see them and to appreciate the gifts and grace they bring to various vocational choices.
- Give them exposure to a variety of forms of ministry through research, observations, and interviewing.
- Help them to view a variety of options before making any commitments to further exploration.
- Once a tentative decision is made, clarify the steps to be taken in order to make that vocational choice a reality.

Maintain confidentiality

- Those inquiring into church-related occupations need the freedom to explore their vocational options without a premature disclosure of their intentions.
- Confidentiality is needed to prevent a premature commitment of a congregation to a candidate. When this occurs, there is always the danger that an inquirer may respond by making a commitment to the wrong vocational choice, or perhaps the right choice for the wrong reasons.
- Confidentiality at the inquiring stage is also essential for those contemplating a career change. Unnecessary pressure is often brought to bear on an employee when it is discovered that she/he is even thinking about changing careers.

Chapter Five

Guidelines for the Pastor/Staff Relations Committee

THE ENLISTMENT, GUIDANCE, AND SUPPORT OF CANDIDATES FOR ORDAINED AND LICENSED ministry in The United Methodist Church is not a responsibility of the clergy alone. It is shared with the pastor/staff parish relations committee (P/SPRC).

The responsibilities of the committee include the following:

To enlist, interview, evaluate, review, and recommend annually to the charge conference lay preachers and persons for candidacy for ordained ministry;

To enlist and refer to the General Board of Global Ministries persons for candidacy for missionary service . . . ;

The committee shall provide to the charge conference a list of students from the charge that are preparing for ordained ministry, diaconal ministry, and/or missionary service, and shall maintain contact with these students, supplying the charge conference with a progress report on each student. (See ¶258.2g(9), 2008 Book of Discipline.*)*

For the sake of the candidates and the enhancement of ministry in The United Methodist Church, this responsibility of the P/SPRC must not be taken lightly. Candidates need the affirmation and support of the committee in order to enter candidacy for ordained or licensed ministry. They need the resources a

P/SPRC can coordinate in the local church for those it recommends. Candidates will also benefit from regular contact with the committee as they prepare to meet the educational and other requirements of their vocational choice.

No one knows the candidate better than the membership of the local church. The recommendation of the P/SPRC committee to the charge conference and, in turn, the recommendation of the charge conference to the district committee on ordained ministry is a crucial gate through which all candidates must pass in order to enter ordained or licensed ministry. It is the one place where the *Discipline* requires the approval of the lay leadership of the local church in the candidacy selection process. It is the one opportunity the local church has to be sure that candidates for ministry meet the criteria and expectations of the local church. If you are concerned about the quality of ministerial leadership in our denomination today, here is the place to address that need.

Finally, let it be noted that although the *Discipline* requires that only candidates for ordained or licensed ministry be enlisted, guided, and supported through the P/SPRC, there is no reason why this committee cannot involve itself in the enlistment of persons for all forms of Christian service. If the committee, the pastor, and the administrative board/council so determine, the committee can have a significant impact on the way the local church looks at the matter of Christian vocation and the quality of people enlisted for all forms of church-related service. Such a task that is done well not only affirms those identified as potential servant leaders, but broadens the vision of the congregation in terms of the nature of Christian vocation. It also awakens the church to the potential that exists for addressing the ministerial needs of the church and gives the local church the satisfaction of knowing that it is playing a significant role in the shaping of ministry for the future.

Guidelines for P/SPRC Members

- Review *The Christian as Minister* with your pastor and other clergy staff, and, if necessary, clarify the role of the committee in the enlistment of candidates for ministry.
- Have the chairperson of the P/SPRC meet with a candidate prior to the meeting where she/he will be interviewed to clarify the purpose of the meeting and the expectations of the committee.
- If a written statement is to be prepared, agree on the form it will take and communicate that information to the candidate.
- The meeting with the candidate may be informal and spontaneous. If the candidate is invited to make a brief oral statement of his/her current decision and interests, the committee members and the candidate may then be free to discuss any issues that seem important.

- While conducting an interview, the committee may wish to keep in mind the historic questions first asked by John Wesley in 1746. These questions apply to anyone seeking to enter candidacy for licensed or ordained ministry.

Wesley's Questions for Examiners

1. *Do they know God as pardoning God? Have they the love of God abiding in them? Do they desire nothing but God? Are they holy in all manner of conversation?*

2. *Have they gifts, as well as evidence of God's grace, for the work? Have they a clear, sound understanding; a right judgment in the things of God; a just conception of salvation by faith? Do they speak justly, readily, clearly?*

3. *Have they fruit? Have any been truly convinced of sin and converted to God, and are believers edified by their service?*

As long as these marks occur in them, we believe they are called of God to serve. These we receive as sufficient proof that they are moved by the Holy Spirit. (¶310, *2008 Book of Discipline*)

The decision of the P/SPRC should be based on more than just the individual's appearance and presentation to the committee. It should also consider how well this person has done in the life of the local church over an extended period of time. This is the reason for the requirement of the candidate having been a member in good standing of a local church for at least two years.

As the committee interviews a candidate for ministry, the following questions may be important:

- In what ways has this person actually experienced God's forgiveness and grace? Does this show in the way she/he lives? How?
- Does this person have personal habits that enhance his/her witness as a Christian? Which personal habits diminish or negate that witness?
- What gifts, skills, abilities does this person have? Can she/he speak clearly and comfortably before a large group and in a small discussion group? What impression or feeling do you get from being with this person? Does this person seem positive, confident, poised, relaxed, open, and friendly?
- How does this person relate to his/her family? Are relatives (parents, siblings, spouse, if any) supportive of the person's candidacy for ministry? Is this person being discouraged by some family members? Why? Do some family members seem to be pushing this person into some form of ministry as a career? In what ways?

- Does this person seem to have the intellectual ability (appropriate to his/her age) to study effectively and work easily with the Bible, theological issues, and the subject matter of the intended career? Has this person had relatively good grades in high school and college (if any)?
- How does this person relate to those in authority, such as church leaders, pastors, managers, teachers, employers, and others who supervise his/her work in some way? Is this person independent, assertive, yet cooperative and pleasant?
- What evidence of effectiveness in church-related leadership has this person already shown? Describe these. To what extent were these the result of this person's initiative and abilities, as compared to being someone else's work that this person merely followed or used?
- What other evidence of future potential has this person shown?
- How committed does this person seem to be to the gospel of Christ and servant ministry in The United Methodist Church? To what extent may salary, prestige, and other rewards be important to this person? How does she/he respond to discouragement, failure, disagreements, and other adverse conditions that are often part of ministry? Will this person be comfortable with the possible restrictions that ministry in the connectional structure of Methodism may impose in some situations?
- What other evidence do you have that the person will enhance and improve the quality of ministry in The United Methodist Church?

Before a candidate is recommended to the charge conference, the chairperson and pastor can encourage the committee members, if they have not already done so, to invite informal, confidential comments from church members and others who know the applicant. If concerns should be expressed about the applicant's fitness for ordained or licensed ministry, the P/SPRC may want to delay making a recommendation to the charge conference until it has time to examine the comments and consult with the applicant about them.

When announcements are made that the charge conference will be voting on a recommendation of candidacy for ordained or licensed ministry, an open invitation should be given to any person who wishes to consult privately and confidentially with the pastor or P/SPRC chairperson about the applicant. In this way it is more likely that varied points of view will be heard and any negative comments will be dealt with in a constructive way.

If potential problem areas do appear from any of these sources, the pastor and the P/SPRC chairperson can decide how to use them in the most constructive manner with the applicant. It may be appropriate to consult with the person offering negative information, delay making a recommendation to the charge conference, or take other action prior to the conference if it is likely that the conference may not be able to handle the issues in a public meeting.

If the announcements of the meeting are made properly and if no serious issues become known that should be handled privately with the applicant, the charge conference meeting provides the public occasion when the church gives its formal endorsement of the applicant.

Charge Conference Recommendation

- The chairperson of the P/SPRC will want to review and emphasize the important decision facing the charge conference. Quoting from some of the *Disciplinary* statements or from the questions suggested for the P/SPRC may help the members present to see the great importance and the challenge of ordained or licensed ministry.
- The chairperson may then offer the candidate the opportunity to make a brief presentation to the conference as a way of introducing or renewing acquaintance with all persons present.
- The chairperson of the P/SPRC should then report on the committee's recommendation to the charge conference, and the reasons for that recommendation should be spelled out in some detail.
- Time may then be allowed for others to comment and present evidence that would support or deny the recommendation.
- The general tone and atmosphere of the conference meeting should be warm, relaxed, and flexible to allow for serious consideration of the decision.
- The charge conference, like the P/SPRC must keep in mind these two objectives in its decision:
  1) To do what is in the best interest of The United Methodist Church and the enhancement of its ministry.
  2) To exhibit a pastoral concern for the individual, regardless of the outcome of the decision.

The P/SPRC must consider ways in which it can maintain its relationship with the candidates it affirms. Candidates for ordained ministry require an annual recommendation from the committee and the charge conference until they become local pastors or provisional members of the annual conference.

For further guidance in the work of the P/SPRC with candidates for ministry, consult the *Guidelines for Leading Your Congregation: Pastor/Staff Parish Relations*, available from Cokesbury.

Appendix

United Methodist Schools of Theology

Boston University School of Theology
745 Commonwealth Avenue
Boston, MA 02215
Web: www.bu.edu/sth

Candler School of Theology, Emory University
202 Bishops Hall
Atlanta, GA 30322
Web: www.candler.emory.edu

Claremont School of Theology
1325 North College Avenue
Claremont, CA 91711-3199
Web: www.cst.edu

Drew Theological School
36 Madison Avenue
Madison, NJ 07940
Web: www.drew.edu/theo

The Divinity School, Duke University
PO Box 90965
Durham, NC 27708-0965
Web: www.divinity.duke.edu

Gammon Theological Seminary
653 Beckwith Street SW
Atlanta, GA 30314
Web: www.gammonseminary.org

Garrett-Evangelical Theological Seminary
2121 Sheridan Road
Evanston, IL 60201
Web: www. garrett.edu

Iliff School of Theology
2201 South University Boulevard
Denver, CO 80210
Web: www.iliff.edu

Methodist Theological School in Ohio
3081 Columbus Pike
Delaware, OH 43015
Web: www.mtso.edu

Perkins School of Theology
Southern Methodist University
PO Box 750133
Dallas, TX 75275-0133
Web: www.smu.edu/theology

Saint Paul School of Theology
5123 Truman Road
Kansas City, MO 64127
Web: www.spst.edu

United Theological Seminary
4501 Denlinger Road
Trotwood, OH 45426
Web: www.united.edu

Wesley Theological Seminary
4500 Massachusetts Avenue NW
Washington, DC 20016-5690
Web: www.wesleyseminary.edu